Montante Family Library
D'Youville College

Women in Church History

20 Stories for 20 Centuries

Joanne Turpin

 St. Anthony Messenger Press
CINCINNATI, OHIO

Nihil Obstat: Rev. Lawrence Landini, O.F.M.
Rev. Robert J. Buschmiller

Imprimi Potest: Rev. Jeremy Harrington, O.F.M.
Provincial

Imprimatur: +James H. Garland, V.G.
Archdiocese of Cincinnati
November 14, 1989

The *nihil obstat* and *imprimatur* are a declaration that
a book is considered to be free from doctrinal or
moral error. It is not implied that those who have
granted the *nihil obstat* and *imprimatur* agree with
the contents, opinions or statements expressed.

Scripture citations are taken from *The New American
Bible With Revised New Testament*, copyright ©1986
by the Confraternity of Christian Doctrine,
Washington, D.C., and are used by permission. All
rights reserved.

Cover and book design by Julie Lonneman

ISBN 0-86716-096-9

©1990, Joanne Turpin

All rights reserved.
Published by St. Anthony Messenger Press
Printed in the U.S.A.

BX 4651.2
.T87
1990

MAR 29 2004

DEDICATED TO MY FAMILY:

Sharon Roberta Turpin,
Patricia Turpin Agouros
AND
George Agouros

CONTENTS

Introduction

Jesus made no secret about his feelings toward women. He gifted them with his healing touch, invited them to be among his disciples and welcomed them as friends. In turn, they supported his mission, followed him along the dark road to Calvary and remained faithfully near the tomb. Jesus rewarded their fidelity with the supreme joy of being the first witnesses to his Resurrection. That's where the story of women in the Church begins—and a glorious beginning it is.

If, in subsequent centuries, historians tended to focus on his-story to the neglect of her-story, blame it on the way they approach their subject. The past has traditionally been described in terms of power struggles, battles of various types—actions and events typically engaged in by men. Such reporting is as typical of Church history as of the secular kind.

Yet, as Franciscan theologian Leonardo Boff observes: "At critical moments it is always the women who show the most courage." If one combs the Acts of Martyrs, the lives of the saints, diaries and biographies written long ago, her-story begins to fall into place.

This book presents 20 women, famous and obscure, each painted against the backdrop of the Church in her century. They were chosen to represent her-story in 20 centuries of Church history according to three criteria: (1) personal holiness, (2) moral courage and (3) the importance of the individual's contribution to the immediate or long-range course of the pilgrim Church.

One of the happier discoveries comes from finding that Jesus (if one may put him in the same category as Christian males) had much company in supporting and encouraging women to use the gifts God gave them and in working in partnership with them. The apostle Paul appears on this list, and so do Boniface and Francis of Assisi and Vincent de Paul and a host of others. Of course it was to their benefit!

In the following pages, women serve as missionaries and martyrs, reformers and peacemakers, pioneers and prophets, teachers and humanitarians, mystics and writers of spiritual literature. They prove that living the Gospel can be done in varied ways, responding to the particular needs of the time and circumstances of life. Once they heard a call from God, nothing—neither official opposition nor family pressure nor even, in some cases, poor health—prevented them from saying yes. They were willing to risk censure, humiliation, even death, in order to answer the call.

From the research into their lives, two messages come across rather vividly.

First, each understood the true meaning of love. This was clearly the motivating force for all: love for the Lord spilling out to encompass humanity. Teresa of Avila perhaps expressed it best: "O my Jesus, how much a soul can do when ablaze with Thy love!"

The power of such love makes an even greater impression when one realizes that society through most of these centuries did not exactly push women to the fore. Nevertheless, with the Lord on their side, how could they go wrong? Sometimes it just took longer to make their point.

A second message these stories give is an emphasis on service, loving service. As an illustration of this, beyond the predictable ways suggested by the term, is the surprising incidence of women washing the feet of others as an act of humble service in imitation of Jesus at the Last Supper. "I have given you a model to follow," he said then, "so that as I have done for you, you should also do" (John 13:15). The women take Jesus literally, doing this in memory of him. They did not regard foot-washing as an act to be reserved as symbolic ritual for a Holy Week liturgy.

Taking Jesus' words to heart has turned ordinary Christians into extraordinary Christians—women as well as men. There's a lesson in that for all of us.

Prisca the Evangelist

BACKGROUND

The Acts of the Apostles vividly describes the first Pentecost. Crowds of Jewish pilgrims had come to Jerusalem for the sacred Feast of Weeks, originally a harvest festival. There they heard Peter preach the Good News—and a rich harvest it turned out to be in terms of converts to faith in Jesus Christ. The converted pilgrims returned to their homes in provinces scattered throughout the Roman Empire to share the exciting news with their Jewish brothers and sisters in diaspora, that is, outside Palestine. (More Jews lived outside biblical Palestine than within its borders at the time.)

Persecution also played a significant role in spreading the faith. When Jewish authorities attempted to stamp out the new sect through persecution, many Christianized Jews sought refuge in Antioch, a city several hundred miles north of Jerusalem. Antioch was where the name *Christian* was first applied to followers of Jesus Christ and also where the conversion of Gentiles in a largely pagan population began in earnest.

In Antioch the apostle Paul—after his own dramatic conversion—joined with Barnabas, a leader in the Church, to preach the message of salvation through faith in Jesus. Their missionary endeavors eventually took them to the nearby island of Cyprus. Later would come travels to other provinces of Asia Minor and, scarcely a dozen years after Jesus' crucifixion, to the European continent.

Other missionaries included John Mark who, according to tradition, authored the second gospel. His mother Mary, one of the early disciples, had opened her home in Jerusalem to fellow believers. This likely was the first house Church, Christians meeting and worshiping together. As Acts 12:12 relates, when Peter was miraculously freed from imprisonment, "he went to the house of Mary, the mother of John who is called Mark, where there were many people gathered in prayer."

Within decades, Mary's house church was to be duplicated in communities across the Middle East and Europe.

CORINTH, A.D. 50

In this noisy, thriving maritime city 40 miles southwest of Athens, a couple from Rome find refuge. Prisca and her husband Aquila are among a group of people expelled from the capital by edict of the Emperor Claudius. He sought by his action to restore public order after a series of sectarian disturbances in certain quarters of the city where synagogues were located. The trouble rages over a man called "Chrestus."

Prisca, a woman of aristocratic background, is believed to be related to the family of Pudens, a well-known Roman senator. According to talk, all the Pudens household has been converted to a new sect known as Christianity, which originated in the East. Aquila's status as a freedman means that, though once a slave, he won freedom either by purchasing or working for it. Marriage of an ex-slave into a family like Prisca's is not uncommon among Romans.

Nobility of birth does not keep Prisca from helping her husband earn a living. The two waste no time in setting up a business in the agora or marketplace of Corinth. Aquila, a tent-maker by trade, weaves or repairs items such as tents, ships' sails and the awnings used over shops.

Corinth offers ample opportunity for trade, situated as the city is on an isthmus linking northern and southern Greece. It also boasts two seaports, one on either side of the isthmus, making Corinth's agora a crossroad of humanity: bankers and sailors, artisans and government officials, philosophers and fortune-tellers.

In the midst of this highly mobile society—and a pagan one at that—Prisca and Aquila not only set up shop but also organize a church in their house like the one they had in Rome. For the two are followers of "the Way" of Jesus Christ and, whenever they find others who share the belief, they invite them to join the community meeting in their home. The couple extend this invitation to their business contacts too, given the chance to steer conversation into more philosophical channels and to explain what Christ's teachings have meant in their own lives.

Christians, as these believers are often called, tend to be viewed with suspicion since their life-style contrasts so sharply with that of the pagan majority. More typical Corinthians take advantage of the diversions—violent gladiator contests, for example, or obscene theatrical performances—that keep them from thinking too deeply about the essential emptiness of their lives. Pagan religion offers little to counteract this poverty of spirit, notwithstanding all the architecturally beautiful temples in and around the agora. Inescapably, greatest attention goes to the temple honoring Aphrodite, goddess of love, which stands on the heights of Acrocorinth, a mountaintop acropolis looming more than 1,800 feet above the city. From the summit, on a clear day, one can see the gleaming temples atop the acropolis in Athens.

For Prisca and Aquila, there is little time for gazing afar, however. After a busy day at the tent-making trade, they spend evenings instructing people more deeply in the faith. Corinthians are a lively lot who sometimes misplace their enthusiasm; special care must be taken to give them a solid, sober grounding in gospel teachings.

At least once a week the little community of believers gathers to celebrate the Lord's Supper: a sacramental breaking of bread and blessing of the cup performed by whoever is designated to preside at the meal. The sacred meal memorializes Jesus' sharing of bread and wine with his disciples at the Last Supper. Along with this sacramental act, the membership reads from scrolls of the Law and the Prophets of Hebrew Scripture—for their faith has its roots in Jewish tradition. Treasured sayings of Jesus are recalled as well, followed by one in the group preaching on the Word. The worship service includes prayers and hymn-singing.

At some time during the accompanying table fellowship (which was a marked feature of Jesus' ministry), they talk of the news from other, similar communities scattered about the provinces of the empire. House churches keep amazingly well informed about each other's activities, for letters can be easily carried by Christian business or missionary travelers going via the expansive network of Roman roads.

Not long after Prisca and Aquila settle in Corinth, news comes in a form even more welcome than letters: this time in the person of Paul, a noted and—as they have heard—often controversial evangelist.

When he arrived from a disappointing sojourn in Athens, Paul went directly to the street of tent-makers in the agora, for finding work in his own trade to support himself is a priority with him. Here he made acquaintance with the couple from Rome, and they immediately invited him to work at the shop and to lodge at their home. For the next 18 months, this close association continued, until missionary work called all of them to another city.

Prisca and Aquila also put Paul in touch with the local synagogue, for he had yet to give up on the idea of convincing his Jewish brothers and sisters that "the Way" is a fulfillment, not a contradiction, of Judaism. Prisca and Aquila think along the same lines, as do many who have committed their lives to following Jesus and continue to attend synagogue services. There one finds not just Jews but also Gentiles (called "God-fearers") attracted to belief in one God as expressed by Judaism.

While Aquila avoids confrontation with his fellow Jews, concentrating his energies instead on guidance of house church members, Paul, who is outspoken by temperament, quickly runs into opposition. As elsewhere, Paul's zeal will eventually lead to trouble.

For her part Prisca, though educated and willing enough to speak wherever she can get a hearing, knows better than even to consider raising her voice at the synagogue gathering. Women there are not allowed a participatory role, let alone permitted to sit alongside their husbands. Only men are counted in determining if the requisite number to conduct a service are present.

When, after a traditional synagogue service on the Sabbath, members of the Christian sect on the next day keep special the Lord's Day, Prisca surely appreciates all the more the egalitarian atmosphere of the house church. For female followers of Christ may pray and prophesy during the service when so moved, and preside over the sacred meal too. (This, in fact, becomes a necessity in communities where women alone constitute the original congregation. Surely that was the case after Paul baptized Lydia and the other women at Philippi—his first converts on European soil.)

As is bound to happen, members occasionally raise the issue of women's visible role or complain at having to share the customary fellowship meal with the mixed social classes typical of a house church. Paul then likes to remind them of a special blessing of their faith (something he put into writing in a letter addressed to the Galatians): "There is neither Jew nor Greek, there is neither slave nor free person, there is not male and female; for you are all one in Christ Jesus" (Galatians 3:28).

Prisca sees clear evidence of his fair-mindedness not just in the way Paul treats her as a coworker, but also in the regard and confidence he places in Phoebe, patroness of a group which meets in her house in the nearby port of Cenchreae, only a three hours' walk away.

In the spring of A.D. 51 everyone looks forward to the popular Isthmian Games, due again in Corinth in April and May. The festival of athletic events and other entertainment, held every two years in honor of Poseidon (god of the sea), draws scores of tourists. With inns limited in number and of poor quality besides, tents are needed to house visitors in the plains surrounding the walled city. This translates into booming business for tent-makers as well as an ideal opportunity to spread the Good News among customers.

Trouble for Paul and his coworkers comes afterward, not for evangelizing the festival's visitors but, rather, for succeeding too well in making converts from among the local population—people the synagogue claims. Jewish leaders zero in on Paul, attempting through court action to get the provincial authority to restrain the man. But the proconsul, Rome's representative in Corinth, refuses to interfere, instead dismissing the case.

At some point after these legal proceedings, the decision is made to move on, for fresh missionary fields beckon. Paul's stay in Corinth actually has been longer than is his habit. When he selects Ephesus, one of the great cities of the empire, as the next destination, there seems no question about his friends and coworkers, Prisca and Aquila, going along too. Since ship movement essentially ceases during the winter months, however, it is not until the spring of A.D. 52 that they depart.

The leisurely 10-day voyage across the Aegean Sea takes them past island scenery of breathtaking beauty. Near the southwest coast of Asia Minor mountains appear through a blue haze, and soon the missionaries are sailing into the inner harbor of Ephesus. Boasting one of the Seven Wonders of the World, the temple of Artemis (goddess of fertility), the city spreads itself out in the foreground of a natural amphitheater.

While Aquila sets up shop in the agora and Prisca readies their newest home to accommodate meetings of Christians already living in Ephesus, Paul spends a brief period trying to woo members of the local synagogue, but with little success. Knowing he leaves the house church in capable hands, Paul goes on to Jerusalem, then visits Antioch and other congregations in Asia Minor which he had founded at an earlier date.

In Ephesus Prisca keeps busy not only preaching the
Gospel but also looking for ways to provide support and
sustenance for the poorer members of her community,
especially the widows. (In the society of that day, widows
often had few resources of their own.) Another feminine
condition that appalls Prisca is the temple-associated
prostitution carried on by young women designated as
priestesses—a common practice in cities of the East.

Paul is still away on his travels when Apollos of
Alexandria comes to town. An authority on Scripture, he
delivers a brilliant commentary at the synagogue, holding
his listeners spellbound. But when he turns to discoursing on
the Way of the Lord, Prisca and Aquila, who are present, find
his knowledge of Jesus incomplete and on many points
incorrect. After the service, they take Apollos home so that
Prisca can instruct him properly.

Apollos accepts with good grace the corrections of this
obviously educated woman. Moreover, he learns that she
hails from the Christian community of Rome. A decade
earlier it had hosted a visit from the apostle Peter and his
wife, who faithfully passed on the teachings of Jesus and
explained in detail how he had fulfilled the biblical prophesy
of the Messiah.

By the time Paul returns to Ephesus, Apollos, armed with
new knowledge, has journeyed on to Corinth to see how he
might fare among its Jews.

The Corinthians are next heard from when emissaries
deliver a message from Chloe, the woman in whose home
the Christians now meet. Problems have surfaced which
require expert advice. What reminiscences Paul and his
companions must have had before he began dictating his
First Letter to the Corinthians, with its elevating words on
the need for love along with down-to-earth admonitions
concerning unseemly behavior at the Lord's Supper.

In Ephesus the conduct of Christians causes trouble, too,
but trouble of a different type. Having earlier witnessed for
their faith by publicly burning expensive scrolls of magic
formulas (the city being a world center for the magic arts),
the Christians next wage a campaign against a vital product

of the silversmith trade: statues of Artemis.

Spring approaches, and with it comes the start of another pilgrimage season when many thousands of devotees of the goddess Artemis converge upon the city. The fervor of pilgrims streaming in from all parts of the empire to visit the temple-shrine is matched by the zeal of local silversmiths who make souvenirs: both replicas of the shrine and silver statuettes of Artemis. The latter—depictions of a many-breasted goddess—prove particularly offensive to Christians. But for the silversmiths, the statuette represents their great money-maker for the year.

When a leading silversmith, Demetrius by name, hears Christians preach against the manufacture of these souvenirs—labeling them idolatrous—he organizes his own protest group made up of fellow artisans. Pilgrims join in the ensuing uproar. Paul and his friends become the target when a near riot takes place at the city's vast open-air theater, though a public official finally manages to cool the high-pitched emotions of the mob.

About the time that order is restored to Ephesus, word comes that Rome has a new emperor. Rumor runs rampant that the previous emperor, Claudius, has been poisoned by his fourth wife. Now, in A.D. 54, her son by a former marriage, Nero, has assumed the throne. It's just the kind of gossip to capture the public fancy. The silversmith episode thus becomes old news.

Since Nero's record contains no opposition to Christianity, Prisca and Aquila feel safe to return to Rome, to their house church on the Aventine Hill, where they will renew acquaintance with old friends and family.

That the couple do resume their role as congregational leaders in the seat of empire is evident from a letter Paul writes later to the house churches in Rome (the number having grown to some half-dozen): "Greet Prisca and Aquila, my co-workers in Christ Jesus, who risked their necks for my life [in the silversmith riot], to whom not only I am grateful but also all the churches of the Gentiles; greet also the church at their house" (Romans 16:3-5).

AFTERWARD

Whether Prisca and Aquila
were among those martyred during Nero's persecution of
Christians in A.D. 64 remains uncertain, though seventh-
century itineraries covering pilgrimage to Rome mention
their burial place in the registry of Roman martyrs' graves.

What is known for certain is the esteem in which Prisca
was held by the early Church. Luminaries such as Tertullian,
Father of Latin theology, and John Chrysostom, a Church
Doctor, give high praise to her work.

Prisca's name—and sometimes Aquila's too—regularly
appears on biblical scholars' lists as a possible author of the
Letter to the Hebrews. (The theme of her instruction of
Apollos, "Jesus is the Messiah foretold in Scripture," is
identical to the main theme of Hebrews.)

A testament to her evangelistic labors is the Church of St.
Prisca, on the Aventine Hill in Rome. An ancient tradition
says it is built over her house of apostolic times. House
churches throughout the empire provided the foundation
for early Christianity.

Around the time of the destruction of the temple in
Jerusalem during a major Jewish uprising against Roman
occupation in A.D. 70, the Christian sect was well on its way to
breaking completely with Judaism.

In following decades, ecclesiastical machinery was
developed to administer an expanding Church. By the
middle of the second century, a manual for Church officers
had been compiled: the *Didache* or "Teaching of the Twelve
Apostles."

Cultural practices of the Greco-Roman world began to
creep in, signified by the fact that women no longer were
seated with men but formed a segregated part of the
congregation. Nevertheless, Christians everywhere felt a
sense of belonging to a universal institution.

Perpetua of Carthage

BACKGROUND

With the death of John the apostle about A.D. 100, the apostolic age drew to an end. After that, it became more important than ever to preserve in writing memories of Jesus' life and teachings as well as apostolic traditions.

Thus, in the second century the process was begun to determine which of the Gospels and other Christian literature circulating in that period were authentic and divinely inspired. By the end of the century, there was general agreement regarding most of the books accepted as part of the New Testament, though the official list did not appear until the fourth century.

Other Christian literature important to this era included that of the apologists: writers who defined and defended the teachings of Christianity in order to counter the verbal and written attacks of pagan intellectuals. One prominent apologist, Irenaeus, became bishop in Lyons (France), replacing the bishop who was martyred in the persecution there in 177. Persecutions so far were sporadic and on a local basis, depending mostly on the whims of the local ruler.

Near the end of the second century, a belief in the imminent second coming of Christ—a belief quite strong during the apostolic age—showed a resurgence, particularly among the faithful in North Africa. That prospect gave the faithful unusual courage.

In the summer of 180 seven men and five women of humble background were brought for trial to the capital city of Carthage from their own township of Scillium. The 12 were found guilty of being Christian and sentenced to beheading. The case of the Scillitan martyrs is history's first mention of the existence of Christianity in North Africa. How it became established is unclear, though one theory suggests that persons fleeing Nero's persecution in Rome may have brought the faith to the region. (Interestingly, Septimius Severus, who became emperor in 193, was of North African origin himself, as was Victor, bishop of Rome in the last decade of the second century.)

CARTHAGE, 180

In the same year in Thuburbo, a suburb of Carthage, a distinguished provincial family celebrates the birth of a girl they name Perpetua. The future looks rosy, for Roman Africa is just entering a period of considerable prosperity, as through the port of Carthage flow the agricultural riches of the provinces along with slaves for the empire.

Growing up in the comfortable and cultured environs of Carthage, Perpetua marries and has a baby of her own. As a young adult, she decides to become a Christian. (One of her brothers appears to have done so too. The rest of the family remains pagan, that is, abiding by the state religion with its nominal belief in patron gods and goddesses.)

Before being initiated into the Christian faith, the aspiring candidate—or catechumen, as one is called—must go through a process of instruction in the faith in addition to following a life of moral rectitude. This testing period lasts an average two to three years, and therefore is not a decision taken lightly, with the obvious result that members remain on the whole a very dedicated people.

For every Christian, the possibility exists of being persecuted by the state for belonging to a sometimes suspect organization. Sporadic persecutions may occur in any province of the empire, perhaps at the whim of the local governor, or due to an outbreak of mob hostility provoked by calamities such as earthquake or epidemic. In an age abounding with superstition, people need a scapegoat and Christians, so markedly different from the rest of the population, serve that purpose.

In the year 202 the empire experiences threats to national security on its frontiers, along with insurrections in various places. Loyalty to the state consequently becomes a paramount issue. Since Christians preach nonviolence to the extent of resisting service in the army, Emperor Septimius Severus decides to issue an edict requiring that all citizens prove their loyalty by making sacrifice to the gods of the empire. This, in effect, amounts to a renunciation of Christianity, with its insistence on belief in only one God.

To clamp down on any further spread of the faith, the edict outlaws efforts to make conversions. In other words, there are to be no more catechumens. The resulting persecution is at its worst in Egypt and North Africa, probably because of the extraordinary fervor of these Christians. (Egypt was always considered a separate region from the North African provinces.)

The arrest of catechumens begins, and Perpetua is among them. She is part of a small group—three men and another woman (Felicitas, a slave in her household)—which is first placed under house arrest. While guarded in a private house for a brief period, the five catechumens manage to be baptized, and their lay instructor, Saturus, voluntarily joins them in confinement. The group is soon moved to the common prison in Carthage.

Perpetua's diary testifies vividly to the sufferings of a young woman from noble background who suddenly finds herself imprisoned even before a hearing on the case has occurred. "I was terrified," she writes, "as I had never before been in such a dark hole. What a difficult time it was!" She tells of the crowded conditions and the stifling heat. But most of all, she is "tortured with worry" because of her infant son.

Perpetua gave the baby over to the care of her mother and a brother when they came to visit her. Later though, she gets permission to keep the baby with her. Without her son, she found the place a "dungeon." But with the baby once more in her arms, it becomes a "palace."

Though Perpetua never doubts that she has made the right decision in refusing to renounce her faith, still she must suffer for the anguish that choice causes her family— particularly her father who, as he reminds her, "favored you above all your brothers." He comes to the prison to plead with her for the sake of her son and for the sake of the family honor. Sadly, she refuses. "Think of your brothers, think of your mother and your aunt, think of your child," he implores. "Give up your pride! You will destroy all of us!"

"This was the way my father spoke out of love for me," Perpetua reflects as she goes on to describe her efforts to comfort him, assuring him that what happens in the prisoner's dock will all happen as God wills. "And he left me in great sorrow." (Neither history nor Perpetua's diary mention her husband or that of her slave Felicitas, who is pregnant.)

While waiting for a hearing and uncertain when it will be, Perpetua reluctantly relinquishes the baby to her father during one of his visits. Then, during breakfast one morning, the prisoners are suddenly hurried off to the forum. In the crowd that quickly gathers, Perpetua sees her father with the baby. He begs his daughter to sacrifice to the gods. To offer incense, a simple statement of loyalty to the empire, seems little enough if it will save her life.

Hilarianus, the official hearing the case, adds his bit: "Have pity on your father's gray head; have pity on your infant son. Offer the sacrifice for the welfare of the emperors."

Perpetua, though, cannot deny her faith in the one true God. "I will not," she says adamantly.

"Are you a Christian?" Hilarianus asks. And she replies, "Yes, I am."

When her father continues pleading with her, Hilarianus

orders him to be thrown to the ground and beaten. For Perpetua it is "just as if I myself had been beaten."

None of the others will recant either. They are sentenced to fight wild beasts in the amphitheater, and then returned to prison to await the scheduled date.

Perpetua hopes that she will be allowed to have the baby with her till the sentence is carried out, but her father refuses. But because the baby no longer needs to be nursed at the breast, she confides to her diary, "I was relieved of any anxiety for my child."

She receives consoling visions, which help her to remain at peace. Saturus, the catechumens' instructor who chose to join them in prison, also keeps a diary. In it he writes of a vision in which he sees their death, and then "when we were free of this world, we first saw an intense light."

All in the group are gladdened to hear about the conversion of the adjutant in charge of the jail. Their greatest concern relates to Felicitas's condition. She fears that she might not be able to die in the arena with the others because of her pregnancy. (Her execution will simply be postponed.) As the time for her delivery draws near, the group prays that it will be soon. Labor pains ensue, and she gives birth two days before the date of execution. Another Christian woman comes forward, taking the baby to raise as her own.

The last meal for the condemned customarily takes place in a room open to the public. The room is filled with spectators as the five companions-in-death turn the occasion into an agape, or love-feast, an early Christian tradition consisting of prayer, a supper and the singing of psalms and hymns. (The shared meal of the agape symbolized the love Christians felt for each other. In apostolic times it had customarily been held in connection with the eucharistic service.) Some of the onlookers ridicule them, but others express only admiration for the dignity with which the group conducts itself that evening.

The rest of Perpetua's story comes to us from an eyewitness account commonly believed to be written by Tertullian, a Carthaginian lawyer turned theologian.

On the morning of March 7, 203, the prisoners are

marched from the prison to the amphitheater, where they will form part of the public entertainment during festivities marking the emperor's birthday. The group goes joyfully, and Perpetua is described as having a "shining countenance and calm step..., putting down everyone's stare by her own intense gaze."

The men are forced to put on the robes worn by priests of Saturn, god of harvests. When the women are given the dress for priestesses of Ceres, a goddess associated with fertility rites, Perpetua resists, arguing with the tribune. He agrees that the women have been told they will not have to wear it.

At the insistence of the spectators, the prisoners are scourged before being mauled by wild animals let loose in the arena. The first two, Saturninus and Revocatus, are attacked by a bear. Perpetua and Felicitas go next, matched against a mad heifer. Stripped naked and put into nets, they are brought into the arena. For a change, the crowd expresses horror at seeing that one of the young women is "fresh from childbirth with the milk still dripping from her breasts." This prompts officials to have the women dressed in tunics.

When Perpetua is tossed into the air by the mad heifer, her tunic rips along the side. More concerned about modesty than her pain, she pulls at the tunic to cover her exposed thighs, then rearranges her disheveled hair. She sees Felicitas in a heap on the ground and hurries over to give her a hand, lifting her up. The two stand side by side, a noble matron and her personal slave, facing death as sisters.

For the moment, the crowd's appetite for violence appears satisfied, and the women are allowed to retreat. Passing near her brother and several catechumens, Perpetua says, "You must all stand fast in the faith and love one another, and do not be weakened by what we have gone through."

Saturus enters the arena last. When the gladiator begins tying the prisoner to a wild boar, he himself is gored by the animal. Saturus is next matched against a bear which refuses to come out of its cage. Finally a leopard is let loose, and with one savage bite drenches Saturus in blood.

Still, the entire group has thus far survived the attacks,

which means they must be put to death by the sword. The mob clamors for the prisoners to be brought into the open where they can witness the bloody spectacle.

Assembling in full view, the five give each other the ritual kiss of peace before each is executed by the sword. Perpetua's turn comes last. The gladiator assigned to dispatch her nervously takes poor aim. His hand slips and the sword strikes bone. Perpetua emits a brief scream, but "then she took the trembling hand of the young gladiator and guided it to her throat."

AFTERWARD

The treasury of early Christian writings was enhanced by a genre of literature known as *The Acts of the Martyrs*. Some of the stories came from official trial records, others from descriptions by eyewitnesses. Still others are obvious embellishments intended to inspire the listener.

The account titled "The Martyrdom of Saints Perpetua and Felicitas" is especially valued as an authentic firsthand narration. Perpetua's diary comprises the greater part, then the account by Saturus. Both introduction and conclusion were composed by an observer at the scene (apparently Tertullian).

During the succeeding 100 years of the empire's periodic and severe persecutions of Christians, the story of Perpetua, one of the early Church's most revered martyrs, would give sustenance to the faithful, drawing them closer together. In recognition of the young woman's sacrifice, her diary was often read during worship services (as were other selections from the *Acts*).

For a number of years, an annual festival honoring her took place at the great basilica in Carthage, where her relics were preserved. The shrine no longer exists and the relics have since been lost, but Perpetua's memory is kept universally alive by the inclusion of her name in the First Eucharistic Prayer. "The blood of Christians is their harvest seed," Tertullian observed. Proof of that was seen in the continued growth of Christianity despite all attempts to eliminate the followers of Christ.

Apollonia of Alexandria

BACKGROUND

With the end of Severus's persecution (he died in 211), Christians in the African part of the empire found themselves blessed with a "long peace," as Church history terms it. Succeeding emperors were busy dealing with other matters, such as Rome's loss of power to control its frontiers. The Church, left undisturbed, used the ensuing four decades to expand its own frontiers: making conversions, defining doctrines and developing ministries in more organized fashion. Bishops, who were chosen by the members of each Christian community, served as a unifying force; ecclesiastical sees kept in contact with each other by letters or at meetings. One synod in Carthage in 220, for example, saw 71 bishops from the provinces of North Africa in attendance.

The long peace notwithstanding, Christians could never become too complacent, for the superstitious pagan population surrounding them was in the habit of blaming Christians whenever things went wrong. And conditions were worsening everywhere—politically, economically and socially. Trouble struck first in Alexandria, signaling that the Christians' era of peace was over.

ALEXANDRIA, 249

In this city on Egypt's Mediterranean seacoast, a mob is incited to torture and puts to death a number of men and women simply because of their identity as Christians.

In a letter to the bishop of Antioch, Dionysius, the bishop of Alexandria, describes the terrible ordeals suffered by members of his congregation. Among the tragedies he recounts: "Next they seized the wonderful old lady Apollonia, battered her till they knocked out all her teeth, built a pyre in front of the city, and threatened to burn her alive unless she repeated after them their heathen incantations. She asked for a breathing space, and when they released her, jumped without hesitation into the fire and was burned to ashes."

As the mob's intentions were clear and since she had no intention of renouncing her faith, Apollonia chose to embrace death voluntarily rather than be dragged into the fire. The early Church esteemed Apollonia both for the courageous way she chose death rather than renounce her faith and for the many years she served the Christian community in Alexandria as a deaconess. So well-known did her record become, a church built in Rome was dedicated in her honor.

Yet, despite acclaim by contemporaries, little of a personal nature regarding Apollonia's life was preserved. Still, a likely picture can be sketched, based on historical information about third-century Alexandria, its Christian community and, in particular, the role of deaconesses. Add to that the wealth of meaning implied in the bishop's description: "wonderful old lady."

At the time of her death, Apollonia was somewhere between 70 and 80 years old. Her birth would have occurred in the latter part of the second century, quite possibly between 170 and 180—roughly the time Perpetua of Carthage was born. Though Apollonia's life spanned parts of two centuries, most of it was lived in the third, a period when the Church entered into significant growth both in terms of organization and as a spiritual force. To look at Apollonia's probable career in Christian ministry is to see the unfolding of ecclesiastical development.

Apollonia survived Emperor Severus's persecution of 203, which took many lives in Egypt as well as North Africa. That same year marked a milestone for Alexandria's Catechetical School; it fell heir to a director named Origen. (Dionysius headed it before becoming bishop.) Under Origen's tutelage, the school was destined to become renowned in intellectual circles. It drew great minds to the Church, including philosophers disillusioned by pagan thinking. This helped to put the faith on a sound theological basis.

Alexandria was the logical place for this to happen. The city had long enjoyed a reputation for learning. It possessed one of the great libraries of the ancient world, with an unrivaled 400,000 volumes.

The Cathechetical School had begun, as the name indicates, for catechumens: men and women receiving instruction for Baptism. Even as the school expanded to cover theological and philosophical courses, both sexes continued to be enrolled as students. Both also performed secretarial duties as amanuenses, trained to take dictation and copy manuscripts by hand. Whether Apollonia ever served in this capacity is not known although, as a deaconess responsible for instructing catechumens, she would have been well acquainted with workings of the school.

By her time the Christian community in Alexandria was long established. According to Western historians, the exact date of the faith's founding is "shrouded in mystery," though the Christian community definitely existed by the second century. Eastern historians, especially the Egyptian Christian ones, trace the beginnings to the arrival of Mark the Evangelist, whom their tradition said founded the first Christian community in Alexandria—always a point of great pride to its faithful. In Mark's day the city's population numbered about one million, a fourth of them Jewish— providing fertile ground for initial conversions. (Tradition says that Mark met martyrdom in Alexandria.)

For a certainty, the faith had taken firm hold in both Upper and Lower Egypt by the end of the second century, when young people like Apollonia were committing themselves to a lifetime of discipleship to gospel ideals. In the midst of an essentially pagan society, they had to wrestle with the difficulties of maintaining high moral standards.

One churchman cautioned the young woman tempted to adopt some of the pagan practices in fashion: "What shall we say of love of ornament, dyed materials, the vanity of colors, the luxury of jewels, gold work, hair waved or curled, eyes mascaraed, eyebrows plucked, rouge, ceruse [a cosmetic containing white lead], dyed hair and all these deceitful artifices?"

Not all temptations proved quite so venial, however. There was, for instance, the social institution of public baths, where mixed nude bathing led to promiscuous behavior by some. Another popular leisure activity, attending the theater, posed problems, too, for performances frequently contained obscene material. In such an atmosphere, the Christian had continually to exert vigilance.

Candidates for acceptance into the faith must prove themselves capable of leading a moral life in addition to going through several years of instruction. In the formation of female candidates, the deaconess played a primary role.

Though the ministry dates back to apostolic times, the deaconess really came into her own during the great expansion of the Church during the third century. Another ministry, the order of widows, also originated in the primitive Church, and during Apollonia's younger years this order still held preeminence. The widows' duties were to pray and to visit the sick. For admission, a woman must be 60 years or older. But great age sometimes meant that a widow was not always able to meet the demands involved in attending to the sick.

As conversions increased, service to the community

became more and more the prerogative of the deaconess, whose ministry went beyond that of the widows to encompass a variety of pastoral, liturgical and educational duties. The deaconess at this time played a more vital part in the Church in the East than in the West, which seemed always reluctant to accept the deaconess as a recognized institution. Alexandria, though a crossroad of the two regions, tended culturally toward the East.

For the female half of Church membership, a woman acting as minister was an absolute necessity in a number of situations in order to avoid any hint of scandal. The sacrament of Baptism had evolved from a simple water ritual into an elaborate ceremony. Early in the third century, Christians began building houses specifically designed for worship. The baptistery, with its pool or cistern, was a major feature. The oldest surviving example of this architecture is in Dura-Europos, Syria. Adult candidates disrobed before stepping into the pool used for the rite. What's more, the anointing of the whole body made it a matter of propriety for a woman to preside during that part of the rite.

Clement of Alexandria, a contemporary of Apollonia, pictures precisely what her role would have been:

> First of all, when women descend into the water
> for baptism, it is necessary that those who thus
> descend should be anointed with the oil of
> unction by the Deaconess....The minister
> normally only anoints the head where women
> are concerned; it is the customary role of the
> Deaconess to anoint the body....When she who is
> baptized comes out of the water, the Deaconess
> shall receive her, instruct her, and look after her,
> to the end that the unbreakable seal of baptism
> may be impressed on her with purity and
> holiness.

The deaconess looked after her charges not just during the baptismal rite but throughout the entire period of candidacy. While the eucharistic liturgy took place on Sunday, catechumens might meet daily with their deaconess for prayer and Scripture instruction, with emphasis on the

Christian way of life. The newly baptized, or neophytes, afterward remained for a time the responsibility of the deaconess.

She proved her worth in other respects too, as Clement further noted: "Where Christian women live in heathen households it is necessary that it should be the Deaconess who goes there and visits women who are sick." Clearly, she inherited the pastoral duty of the order of widows. At the eucharistic liturgy the deaconess functioned as doorkeeper, standing at the entrance to the women's section and making sure that decorum was maintained.

All Christians, not only special ministers such as the deaconess, had an enviable reputation among the surrounding pagan society on account of the extraordinary spirit of love they demonstrated in caring for the poor and the sick, whether of their own faith or not. During epidemics, when pagan households in dread of contagion put their ailing and dying members into the street, the victims were routinely rescued by Christians.

Yet despite such heroic witness, the minority inevitably came in for mistreatment themselves whenever people's fears were exploited. As conditions in the empire worsened, the government saw a need once more to underscore a mood of patriotism, traditionally solidified behind the state religion. A year before the Emperor Decius's edict requiring citizens to prove loyalty by sacrifice to state gods, a pagan priest in Alexandria stirred up the mob that brought about Apollonia's martyrdom as well as that of many others. That "wonderful old lady"—one of the countless to whom the Church owes its survival—would receive universal recognition for the final act of her long lifetime of service, as we have seen, because one bishop happened to write a letter to another bishop.

AFTERWARD

The year following Apollonia's death, the short but severe Decian persecution was the first systematic effort of the imperial administration to wipe out the Church. After that, as before, periods of relative peace for Christians alternated with times of trouble. By far the worst empire-wide persecution was launched in 303, during Diocletian's reign as emperor. Egypt bore the brunt, with a reported 144,000 Christians put to the sword. Even so, by early in the fourth century, Christians constituted the majority of the population in Egypt. The faith had been firmly rooted by servants of the Church such as Apollonia.

When the new Emperor Constantine granted freedom of worship in 313, abruptly changing the fortunes of the faith, asceticism and consequent celibacy began to take the place of martyrdom as the "highest call" to discipleship.

Once the religion was state-approved, conversions came in greater numbers than ever before, making impossible the lengthy, individualized process of instruction. The shift to baptizing the very young rather than waiting for adulthood further lessened the need for the deaconess. Ministry was on its way to being associated with male priesthood.

Monasticism increasingly seemed almost the sole outlet for the woman eager to dedicate herself to the service of God, although the female diaconate continued to function as part of the ecclesiastical structure for some time yet in the eastern half of the Church.

The Fourth Century

Macrina of Cappadocia

BACKGROUND

Won over to the faith, Emperor Constantine took an active role, convening the first ecumenical council in the history of the young Church. Some 300 bishops from around the empire accepted the invitation, though the aging bishop of Rome declined, sending two representatives in his stead. Meeting in Nicaea (northwest Asia Minor) in 325, the council's primary intention was to do something about a controversial priest in Alexandria named Arius, who was preaching that Christ was only human and not the Son of God. Constantine banished the priest, and the council formulated the Nicene Creed. The heretical doctrine itself was not as easily disposed of as Arius. In fact, when Constantine finally accepted Baptism on his deathbed in 337, the rite was performed by an Arian bishop.

A year or two after the council, Constantine sent his mother Helena, then in her late 70s, on a mission to the Holy Land to verify the sites made sacred by Jesus' life. As a result of her work, a spiritual force was unleashed and pilgrimage to the holy places became the goal of devout Christians.

In 330 Constantine moved the capital of the empire from Rome to Constantinople, building a city named, of course, in his honor over the site of ancient Byzantium. This move to a more geographically defensible position shifted the empire's base of influence eastwards. Among the centers of trade in

the East was the city of Caeserea. And among the city's
distinguished families was that of Basil the Elder.

CAESEREA, c. 340

"Many men wanted to marry
her on account of the reputation of her beauty." So wrote
Gregory of Nyssa in *The Life of St. Macrina*. He surely knew,
for Gregory's subject was his sister. (Elsewhere he praised
her intellect and sanctity.)

At this time Macrina is about 12 or 13, the customary age
when parents arranged marriage for a daughter. Although
she has no desire for marriage, Macrina accedes to her
father's wishes. His choice for her is a young man of great
promise, one already noted as an orator and a defender of
the "wronged" in lawsuits. But before the wedding
ceremony can take place, the man dies unexpectedly.

Macrina's father, Basil the Elder, would have chosen
another fiancé for her. But this time she resolves to follow her
own design, made before the ill-fated betrothal: to live as a
consecrated virgin while remaining at home as companion
to her mother. Although Basil is a skilled lawyer, he finds his
daughter's counterargument persuasive: that she cannot
marry another, for her "husband" is merely absent, away on
a journey to God, and she must "keep faith with an absent
husband." Her novel reasoning gets support from her
mother, Emmelia, who before Macrina's birth learned in a
vision that her firstborn would be a special child. Basil must
share that view, for Macrina wins her case.

Shortly after, Basil dies, leaving Emmelia with 10
children. Macrina, as the oldest, immediately takes over the
care of the youngest, infant Peter, in addition to sustaining
her mother in her grief. Fortunately they have no financial
worries, for the family owns landed estates in three
provinces. Despite her age, Macrina proves adept in the
management of business affairs. And even though the

household is staffed with servants, she doesn't neglect domestic chores either. She shows remarkable skill in spinning wool and "making bread for her mother with her own hands," as Gregory admiringly relates. Above all, Macrina passes on to her five brothers and four sisters the principles of a good moral life, drawing on the solid grounding in Scripture provided by her parents since her early childhood. Gregory remembers that she was "my teacher in all things."

Once the children are grown, the family wealth is apportioned among them. (Naucratius, the brother dearest to Macrina, has in the interim died in an accident while helping the poor.) Arrangements are made for the four sisters—presumably marriage. Gregory refers to them in only the briefest way. Finally Macrina's longed-for dream is about to come true.

In the preceding years, she has gradually led her mother along the path to a contemplative life-style. Now, around the year 355, she persuades Emmelia to establish an ascetic community of women on one of the family estates: at Annesi, a pastoral setting on the Iris River in Pontus, the province north of Caeserea.

According to plan, they take the household maids, who will live with them as sisters in this new arrangement, sharing the same food, accommodations and manual labor. They will share too as equals in the spiritual life, to be fostered by asceticism and prayer. There are, in fact, two branches of the community slated: one for women and another for men, with the youngest brother Peter included among the latter.

The history of a consecrated life for women began with the New Testament "order of widows": older women committed to lives of chastity, prayer and good works within their Christian congregation. It wasn't long before younger women were able to become deaconesses.

Many chose to consecrate themselves to virginity. Various ways of living out that radical commitment developed: Some remained "in the world" but wore black or gray to set them apart from other unmarried women.

Consecration might consist of a church ceremony in which the bishop bestowed a blessed veil, or be made publicly visible when the hair—a woman's "glory" was shorn as an act of renunciation. Whether living at home or with a small group of other consecrated virgins, the women would fast, pray and labor—much like contemplative nuns today.

History tells us that Antony of Egypt, venerated as the "Father of Monasticism," left his younger sister in the care of a community of ascetic virgins before taking up the life himself in the desert about 275. (There were at the time no similar institutions for men.)

Early in the fourth century another Egyptian, Pachomius, expanded on Antony's concept but emphasized the community aspect of monasticism. His sister Mary was eager to grow in the spiritual life too, and soon the desert flourished with communities of nuns as well as monks. It was about the year that Mary's first convent was established near Tabennisi when Macrina made her initial decision. Because her family then lived in Caeserea, a major city of the empire, they undoubtedly heard of events transpiring in the "Holy Land," as people called Egypt in honor of the thousands of devout men and women intent on recapturing the gospel ideal of lives spent in love and service to each other.

Following the Peace of Constantine and the end of persecution, Christianity found itself becoming the state religion. As a result, the Church tended toward increasing involvement in politics and other secular matters. Monasticism originated as a lay movement in opposition to this growing worldliness.

Macrina's style of monastic life at Annesi differs from the Egyptian model in several respects. The most obvious is the physical environment: woods and valleys rather than desert sands. But more importantly, in her version the monastic community reaches out to the broader community around it, engaging in works of mercy. For example, Macrina goes out and literally picks up women lying on the road in a state of starvation. (Unless a woman was independently wealthy or provided for by father, brother or husband, her well-being remained at risk.) After being nursed back to health, those rescued seem glad to stay on as members of Annesi. And whatever their age, they call Macrina "mother."

Charitable works are another feature of her monastery. She establishes a hospital for the poor in connection with Annesi. When a terrible famine strikes this part of the world, no one who comes for help is turned away due to brother Peter's foresight in storing up provisions. "The large numbers going to and fro," writes Gregory, "makes the hermitage seem like a city."

While Peter has from the start worked alongside his sister and mother, Gregory has married and Basil has established a school of rhetoric in Caeserea. Basil, because of Macrina's inspiration and persuasion, as he would later recount, decides to join her monastic endeavor. Before doing so, however, he makes a tour of communities in Egypt and Syria, then returns to govern the men's quarters at Annesi as abbot. He stays only a few years, however, before going back to the city to aid the bishop in fighting the heresy of Arianism.

In that sojourn as a monk, Basil—"the Great" is the title his later prominence would confer on him—devises a rule of life for monks still used by the Eastern Orthodox Church. When he becomes bishop of Caeserea in 370, Basil continues to follow his sister's example, founding charitable institutions, including a hospital for the poor similar to the one at Annesi.

Gregory too succumbs to Macrina's appeals, gives up the secular life and is ordained a priest. (His wife may have already died. In any case, celibacy is not yet mandatory.) Like Basil, he engages in fighting Arianism, a doctrine denying the divinity of Christ, and enjoys the distinction of being one of the leading theologians in the East.

After her mother's death, about 370, Macrina gives all her wealth to the poor. The center at Annesi must, therefore, support itself solely by its own labor, earning income through handwork such as spinning (one of Macrina's domestic achievements as a girl) and sometimes copying manuscripts.

The convent continues to grow because of the attraction it holds: giving women an opportunity to use their gifts. Society otherwise allows them little in the way of self-development. Neither does the Church utilize their talents in ministry as in pre-Constantine times. Current thinking regarding women's capabilities in comparison to that of men's is manifest from the very first page of Gregory's *Life* of his sister: "We speak of a woman, if one may refer to her as that, for I do not know if it is right to use that natural designation for one who went beyond the nature of a woman."

Gregory's most lavish praise for his beloved sister is prompted by a visit to her on his return from an important Church gathering in Constantinople. He has not seen Macrina for some years because of difficulties arising from his courageous defense of the faith; he suffered exile when pro-Arian rulers sat on the throne.

Their brother Basil died only a few months before, and now Gregory is grieved to find his sister seriously ill. He also becomes fully cognizant of her "angelic existence" at Annesi. Despite a feverish state, she continues to live as always: sleeping on a board laid on the ground, with another board as her pillow.

They speak of Basil's death and, in the course of an extended discussion, Macrina expresses lofty thoughts on death and the resurrection of the soul which will serve as the basis for Gregory's great work, *On the Soul and the Resurrection*. (He is careful to give her credit.)

After a while, Macrina tells her brother that surely he must be weary from his long journey and advises him to get some rest.

When later their conversation is resumed, he begins to complain of his problems with the pro-Arian Emperor Valens and of all the disputes within the Church he is constantly called on to settle due to his prominence. She scolds him, telling Gregory that his fame is not due to anything on his part but "that prayers of your parents," she says, "are lifting you to the heights, since you have little or nothing within yourself by which to achieve this." (In times past, she had likewise straightened out their brother Basil who, as a young man, was "puffed up" with pride.) Evidently Gregory accepts her words with humility, since he records them.

In his sister's last hours, Gregory continues to be inspired by her example: "It was as if an angel had by some providence taken on human form."

Later, making funeral preparations, Gregory asks for some burial attire other than her simple gown and worn sandals. Learning that this is all she has, so austerely did she live, he covers her body with his episcopal cloak. Finally, Gregory witnesses the affection in which Macrina is held as shown by the tremendous grief of both the Annesi community and the crowds of mourners who come from all parts of the province.

AFTERWARD

In a family remarkable for the number of saints it produced—Macrina's mother, father, grandmother (Macrina the Elder), three brothers—Macrina is the one dubbed holy and great. For the Eastern Church she provided the model for a women's religious community. The "spiritual kingdom" of the convent promised intellectual as well as spiritual growth and, incidentally, escape from the arranged and often unwelcome marriage. Asceticism was a small price to pay for such gains.

Macrina pioneered further in developing the concept of social welfare in connection with monasticism, an idea picked up by the Church in the West and one of inestimable value for the future.

In a golden age of writings by Church Fathers, supporters behind the scenes often were sisters, mothers or female friends. Take for example Jerome, noted for translating the Bible into Latin. Late in the fourth century, he and some from his circle of noble Roman ladies went to

Bethlehem, where he wrote while they served as helpmates and also founded monastic houses.

Back in the Roman monastic circle, women did scholarly Scripture studies, though none of the writings was apparently preserved. Macrina's voice, of course, is heard through the work of her famous brothers. Proof of what women were capable of may be seen in Egeria's *Diary of a Pilgrimage*. Of independent means, highly literate and perhaps a nun, she journeyed widely through Egypt, Syria, Palestine and beyond, leaving an account of her travels to churches, shrines and monasteries. The manuscript, which was discovered in a library in Italy only a century ago, provides valuable data on liturgical practices in the East at the turn of the century (c. 400).

The Fifth Century

Pulcheria of Constantinople

BACKGROUND

Like his predecessors, Theodosius the Great was a Roman emperor who involved himself in Church business—but not just to engage in weighty matters such as stamping out Arianism and other heresies. Theodosius also got down to the finer points of ecclesiastical administration. In 390, for example, he issued a decree that forbade women to come to church if, "contrary to human and divine law," they were so bold as to cut their hair. There were even sanctions against the bishop who allowed a shorn woman to attend church. To Theodosius's credit, he was willing to apply standards of obedience to himself as well. Once when ordered to do public penance by a bishop for an act judged sinful, he complied.

Imperial standards were lowered when his son Arcadius succeeded him to the throne at Constantinople in 395. During Arcadius's reign the revered John Chrysostom became patriarch (archbishop) of Constantinople, a leading position in the Church at large. After incurring the enmity of the emperor's wife Eudoxia, John was stripped of his episcopacy. The weak-willed Arcadius sat back while Eudoxia managed the ugly business, allying herself with the patriarch of Alexandria, who had earlier had a run-in with the fearlessly upright John Chrysostom. Byzantine politics, secular or ecclesiastical, were messy.

CONSTANTINOPLE, JULY 4, 414

Arcadius's 15-year-old
daughter Pulcheria ascends the throne to act as regent and
guardian for her younger brother, Theodosius II. Since their
father's death in 408, the Roman Empire has been without its
traditional emperor. Although a minister of state has
governed well during the interim (their mother's death
predated the father's), the people long for royalty to lead.
And since Pulcheria shows such a grasp of affairs, she is
chosen to take the reigns of government till her brother, two
years younger, acquires the necessary maturity.

Pulcheria's grandfather, Theodosius the Great, had
earlier divided the Roman Empire into East and West; each
half was governed by one of his sons. When invasion by
Teutonic tribes seemed imminent, the capital in the West was
moved to Ravenna. Now only the bishop of Rome remains to
keep order in that beleaguered city. Constantinople, in a far
more secure position, has grown to be the center of power
and wealth for the empire.

Pulcheria has no easy job, ruling from a city known for its
political plots and counterplots, corruption and high
passions. In one of her first public acts, performed in the
Great Church of Constantinople, she vows to live within the
precincts of the royal court as a consecrated virgin. Her two
younger sisters vow the same. Compared to the recent past,
when their parents' life-style was described as "riotous," the
new atmosphere makes the palace seem almost monastic.

Brother Theodosius and the three sisters fast twice a
week, study and pray. The young women forsake cosmetics
and extravagant dress. Pulcheria's piety extends further—to
building churches, establishing shelters for the homeless,
founding monastic communities and providing for their
support from her personal fortune.

In a court ever hungry for scandal, Pulcheria takes great

care to avoid even a hint of it. She does not speak with any man save in public places. By refusing to marry, she avoids others' ambitious schemes to create political alliances that may not be best for the empire—or for her brother's position. Though Theodosius bears the title of emperor (hers is the imperial *Augusta*), he lacks Pulcheria's shrewdness—or "manly spirit," as the historian Gibbon will later put it. Rather, he prefers such pursuits as hunting and painting, and depends on his sister to exercise power for the royal family. His education has also been entrusted to her, and she oversees this with typical thoroughness. Theodosius emerges well-educated, but his vacillating nature remains the same.

Reaching the age of 20, he asks Pulcheria to find him a bride, stressing that beauty ranks before all else, even before royal background. None in the female population of Constantinople suits him. Instead he falls in love with Athenais, the beautiful and intelligent daughter of an Athenian philosopher. After she has been baptized a Christian and her pagan name changed to Eudokia, the wedding takes place.

For a time after that Pulcheria goes on administering state affairs while Eudokia is occupied with domestic matters, giving birth to a girl in 422. The following year her adoring husband grants Eudokia the title *Augusta*, the same title previously given Pulcheria. Eudokia begins to resent the influence her sister-in-law has over Theodosius, and trouble is not long in coming. Sharing the same palace roof becomes impossible. And so Pulcheria decides to ease the situation by moving, along with her sisters, to one of their suburban palaces, where the three continue to live ascetically while engaging in many philanthropic works.

Pulcheria, however, does not abandon her interest in state affairs, or ecclesiastical ones either. In the Church of the East, debate over religious matters is practically a national pastime. Butcher, baker and just about everyone else—all consider themselves amateur theologians. Passions rise and quarrels erupt into fistfights.

One of the most emotionally-charged subjects is the

Blessed Virgin, a figure deeply revered by the majority. When in 428 a priest preaches the impossibility of a human becoming "Mother of God," he provokes a near-riot in the church where he speaks. Nevertheless, Nestorius, the Patriarch of Constantinople, takes up the idea, arguing that Mary should be called Christ-Bearer, not God-Bearer. (Theologians of the period accept Church teaching that Jesus was both human and divine, but the relationship between the two natures has yet to be defined.)

Battle lines are quickly drawn, hardened the more by Nestorius's dogmatic position. Into the fray steps Eudokia, who lines up with the patriarch. Upholding the opposite, orthodox view, Pulcheria is joined by a leading light in the Church, Cyril, Patriarch of Alexandria. Both sides accuse the other of heresy, while Theodosius squirms uncomfortably in the middle. (The emperor's voice is expected to be the controlling one in Church matters.)

He wavers between wife and sister. The winner is evident when Theodosius calls a general council of bishops to meet at Ephesus in 431 and Cyril is chosen to preside. The council proclaims Mary the "Mother of God." Nestorius is forced to step down as patriarch and banished to Egypt.

Seeing Pulcheria as engineering the defeat of Nestorius, his partisans initiate a campaign of slander against her (though she wins praise from Pope Leo the Great). Theodosius apparently pays no attention to the scurrilous rumors, for he and his sister proceed to work on projects of importance, such as the compilation into 16 volumes of the Theodosian Code of Law, later a basis for much legislation in Western Europe.

Eudokia, meanwhile, is busy with a project of her own: arranging the marriage of her only daughter to the emperor of the West, thereby uniting the two royal families. But following this triumph, trouble appears to rise between her and Theodosius. Some speculate it is because of her inability to bear a son.

In early 438 Pulcheria, to make amends for her late mother's ill treatment of the holy John Chrysostom (whose criticism of the woman's morals had led to his exile and death), arranges to have his body returned and buried with honor in a Constantinople church. It is a highly popular move. We find no mention that Eudokia is present at the ceremony. Soon after, she leaves for a pilgrimage to the Holy Land, ostensibly in thanksgiving for her daughter's happy marriage.

Upon her return a year later, a very ambitious court eunuch named Chrysaphius conspires with the politically inexperienced Eudokia to turn Theodosius against his sister and eliminate Pulcheria's influence. (In the Byzantine Court it was not unusual for a eunuch, perhaps originally employed as an attendant to the emperor, to advance to a position with significant powers, such as palace chamberlain.)

Part of the plot involves having Pulcheria ordained a deaconess, for that function will exclude her from any role in government. One of Pulcheria's allies in the hierarchy warns her, and she promptly retires to her palace in Hebdomon to avoid ordination. But this leaves the way open for Chrysaphius to gain full control over the well-intentioned but weak-willed Theodosius.

Pulcheria's one source of power remains that of a holy woman, for so the people of Constantinople regard her. (In fact, a bishop has her image painted above the altar of the Great Church.)

Though adept at gaining power, Chrysaphius shows himself no match for Pulcheria in managing the empire's business, which suffers as a result. Another theological crisis will plague him. That trouble starts with his godfather Eutyches, the superior of a monastery who also enjoys a favored position at court, for he is among those under the protection of the eunuch.

Eutyches previously led the most violent opposition to Nestorianism. Gradually he comes to advocating the idea that Christ's humanity was absorbed in his divinity: a proposition labeled Monophysitism, or belief that Jesus had only one nature.

When Flavian, now Patriarch of Constantinople, deposes Eutyches for his teaching, the latter appeals for help.

Theodosius is prevailed upon to convene another general
council of the Church at Ephesus in 449. At a chaotic
gathering, soldiers compel those in attendance to vote the
way of Eutyches (and his sponsor, Chrysaphius)—causing it
to be called "the Robber Council." Flavian is roughed up
before he is deposed as patriarch and imprisoned, where he
dies. Theodosius upholds the council's decision, and
Pulcheria for the moment is helpless to do anything despite
appeals from Pope Leo in Rome.

But Chrysaphius's days are numbered, for Theodosius
decides he has had his fill of a poorly managed empire. In the
spring of 450 he recalls his sister to resume administration of
the government. Just a few months later, when Theodosius's
fall from a horse proves fatal, Pulcheria becomes sole ruler of
the empire—the first woman ever to do so.

Understanding the prudence of governing with a
husband at her side in the present circumstances, she
arranges to marry Marcian, a general of stellar reputation,
who agrees to respect his wife's vow of virginity. The two see
eye to eye on politics, both civil and ecclesiastical. Moving
swiftly to deal with the divisive effects of "the Robber
Council," the royal couple calls another general council.

Meanwhile the Huns threaten to invade, and Marcian
hastens to the battlefield to take personal charge. Pulcheria,
no stranger to councils, handles the arrangements. She
selects as the assembly hall the Basilica of St. Euphemia at
Chalcedon (near the capital) both for its accommodating size
and because she trusts in the protection of that female
martyr.

On October 8, 451, more than 500 bishops—representing
all the provinces of the Eastern Empire as well as four legates
from Rome—begin their work. Once the business of
Eutyches and the scandalous situation surrounding the
meeting in 449 is disposed of, the council proceeds with the
task of defining the nature of Jesus Christ—a doctrine still
standing more than 1,500 years later. The definition, based
on a letter written by Pope Leo, explains how Jesus' two
distinct natures, human and divine, exist in one person.

When Marcian, back from the battlefield, appears before

the bishops with Pulcheria, the two are acclaimed. She receives additional praise from the pope for being instrumental in restoring harmony to the Church.

AFTERWARD

Following her death two years later, all of Pulcheria's personal wealth was distributed to the poor in accordance with her wishes. Her legacy to the bishop of Rome was beyond price. Through her efforts, she had helped preserve mainstream Christianity, and by the use of Pope Leo's *Toma* (letter) as basis for the doctrine of Christ's nature, strengthened his position. (In another letter, a personal note to Pulcheria, Leo wrote: "I give thanks to God when I see how you commit yourself to every concern of the universal Church.")

In the past, rivalry among the patriarchates of Alexandria, Antioch, Constantinople, Jerusalem and Rome had been intense as they jousted for lead positions in the Church. Two chief power centers emerged from Chalcedon: Constantinople and Rome. But the patriarchate of the former was destined to become more and more a political tool (future sovereigns would not be so dedicated as Pulcheria), and so its ecclesiastical strength was diluted.

As the political empire of the West came crashing down in 476, the Church remained the only institution left to help civilization survive the Dark Ages descending upon the continent. As the only figure of authority, the head of the Church in Rome out of necessity assumed temporal as well as ecclesiastical rule. The papacy, in terms of authentic power, is sometimes said to have begun with Pope Leo.

One sad footnote to Chalcedon: not everyone accepted the council's declarations. Among those refusing was the Egyptian Church. Part of the problem stemmed from a misunderstanding caused by language differences. Some of the resistance also had to do with nationalistic feelings.

Egyptians resented having to be subservient to foreign rule—
that is, Constantinople—because the Byzantine Empire, as it
was now being called, still held sway over Egypt.

Brigid of Kildare

BACKGROUND

Around the time that St. Patrick was growing up in Britain, the last of the Roman legions departed its soil. Rome could no longer afford the expense of defending the far reaches of the empire. At age 16, Patrick left Britain too, though not willingly. His native Britons, representing what Christianity existed, lived in the interior—pushed there by invading Angles, Saxons and Jutes from northern Europe. Patrick was carried off by raiders to be sold as a slave to an Irish master; he worked in Ireland as a shepherd for six years before making his escape. Though much of Patrick's life is wrapped in legend, it appears that, once free, he decided to be a priest like his grandfather.

After training for Holy Orders in Gaul (France), Patrick chose to return to Ireland, this time as a missionary. Owing to the admirable Irish tolerance of new ideas, even religious ones, missionaries to that country never seemed to be candidates for martyrdom. When Patrick appeared on the scene in the mid-400's, there were already traces of Christianity. With his knowledge of the language and culture, along with a gift of persuasion, he made great headway. It has been suggested by some scholars who see similarities in religious practices that Egyptian monks may have made missionary journeys to this far western end of

Europe. It's also been said that Ireland, till then having
escaped any large-scale invasions, was not conquered until
the Irish surrendered to Christianity.

KILDARE, IRELAND, c. 500

Brigid, abbess of a
flourishing monastery in the valley of the River Liffey,
decides she needs help and invites her friend Conleth to join
her. With a group of followers, he has been leading an ascetic
life in the neighborhood. Brigid convinces him to accept
consecration as a bishop so that he can provide her
establishment with the ecclesiastical services only a bishop
can give. Conleth and his monks move to a site adjacent to
her convent, creating a double monastery, the only known
example in Ireland.

Brigid's power of persuasion had become evident early
in life—a life that began about the year 450 in a place called
Faughart on the east coast of Ireland. Her father, Dubthach,
was chieftain of one of the country's numerous petty
kingdoms, and her mother, Brocessa, served as a slave in his
household.

When Dubthach's jealous wife insisted that he get rid of
Brocessa, she was sold to a Druid who lived on the other side
of the country. A Christian like her mother, Brigid spent her
early years in the home of a pagan priest. Although the Irish
were turning increasingly to the Christian faith, the Druid
religion still claimed many adherents—Brigid's father
among them.

At about age 10, Brigid decided to return to her father's
home, where she promptly upset the household with an
unbreakable habit of giving away food, clothing and other
family goods to the poor.

One day, after getting word that her mother was ailing
and could use a hand with the work, Brigid crossed back to
the opposite coast, apparently not bothering to obtain her

father's permission. Once more with the Druids, this time as a dairymaid, she continued to be as bountiful as ever, dispensing the master's butter, milk and cheese to the needy. But the girl's winning personality combined with her industriousness seemed to keep the master from despairing over her liberality.

In the meantime, despite Brigid's unconventional ways, her father had not given up on her. When she reached marriageable age, Dubthach went to great lengths to find exactly the right man for her. Extolling her assets—health, beauty, intelligence and a willingness to work—he produced a youth not only of exemplary character but, even more praiseworthy, a poet. At this time, the bard enjoyed an exalted position in Irish society. Brigid would have lacked for nothing, including prestige. But the strong-willed young woman refused. Chieftain her father might be, but he was powerless when she overruled him.

While Dubthach aimed high for his natural daughter, her aim was higher: "Since I first fixed my mind on God," she once said, "I have never taken it off." Regardless of the fact that no convents existed for women, Brigid decided to consecrate her life to God. (There had been monastic settlements for men since before Patrick's recent missionary endeavors.)

True to character, once Brigid had a dream, she wasted no time in making it become reality. First, though, came the matter of her mother's circumstances. As a woman in bondage, Brocessa possessed no rights. A slave is the property of the master, who owns her body and soul. But the resourceful Brigid, capitalizing on the fact that to give slaves their freedom is considered a magnanimous act, convinced the Druid master to set Brocessa free. Once she had her mother situated more favorably, Brigid was free to proceed with plans for her own future.

In Irish society then, women desiring to live as consecrated virgins did so at home, devoting their days to prayer, works of mercy and the weaving of vestments and altar cloths. Families, especially those not Christian, often failed to understand—which made the life difficult.

Brigid found seven women of like mind, and together they approached a bishop named Maccaile, who agreed to accept their vows as nuns. Brigid and companions, dressed in simple white habits, made their profession about 469 in a ceremony at Westmeath, in the Midlands of Ireland. Bishop Maccaile draped a white cloak about Brigid's shoulders and a white veil on her "yellow locks," as tradition describes her hair. Ignoring her youthful age, he authorized Brigid to head Ireland's first convent. The site for it, his gift, was at a place called Croghan Hill.

For her part, Brigid had to see to the actual building of the convent. In religious settlements in the country, living space for community members typically consisted of a series of "cells." The cells, or huts, generally of clay and wattle, were constructed in the shape of a beehive—perfect for shedding rain in the moist climate. The earthen floors were strewn with rushes to ensure both warmth and cleanliness. Even the church—though the main building—was ordinarily of modest proportions and built of wood. The whole was then enclosed by walls of earth or stone, much as Irish chieftains designed their fortress-headquarters.

Once settled in, the nuns did not settle back, for a monastic colony is meant to be self-supporting as well as prayer-filled. The women farmed the fields surrounding the enclosure; and when that work was done, they kept occupied with spinning and embroidery. (The Irish prized handwork of all kinds.) In addition, the convent offered asylum to anyone in need.

Brigid and the seven other nuns—who seem to have remained lifelong, loyal companions—soon found that more cells must be added to accommodate others desirous of this new and stimulating kind of life where holiness can be developed along with a woman's talents.

Once the pioneering monastery is in full swing and running smoothly, Brigid eagerly goes about the business of setting up similar foundations in other parts of Ireland. With a nun or two to accompany her, she begins to journey the length and breadth of the country: crossing rivers, meadows and bogs, traveling roads that are little more than a track.

The usual transportation, a two-horse chariot, is driven either by a laborer in her employ or sometimes by the chaplain of one of her settlements, though she can handle the chariot too.

She sees her apostolic work well-rewarded as the land blossoms with new communities for women. Just as Patrick before her had attracted converts and founded monasteries (though only for men), Brigid too enjoys the gift of drawing people to herself. (Whether the two ever met is debatable, since Patrick died when she was still a child.)

Christianity's appeal to the Irish may be owing not only to a natural fervor but also to an inherent love of learning. In the "colleges" of Celtic tradition, poets might spend a dozen years in disciplined study of the extensive, rich Celtic literature in oral form. Patrick had brought with him on the missionary trail a written language using the Latin alphabet. This contribution to his adopted land, whose heritage included a reverence for words, was a treasure indeed.

Happily, the Christianized chieftains donate land for Church use, and as monastic colonies flourish, so too does their growing reputation as centers of learning. Women as well as men participate in this outburst of education, which is not limited to study of Scripture and the Church Fathers. For the converted Irish never turn their backs on their native culture; they preserve the best. Neither do they neglect the secular classics of Western civilization.

At the same time, Europe's troubles are multiplying due to invasions and mass migrations of Goths, Vandals and other tribes. For safety's sake, monks flee the continent to Ireland, bringing with them irreplaceable manuscripts from their monasteries and valuable pieces of art too.

The Irish set about creating some great art of their own, as well. Brigid's premier foundation at Kildare, for instance, specializes in the production of manuscripts. In the scriptorium, nuns and monks illuminate parchment pages with superb illustrations, border designs and richly decorative capital letters—all done in sumptuous colors and gold leaf. In order to preserve learning, they laboriously hand-copy page after page of academic and religious texts.

While today the eighth-century *Book of Kells*, an illuminated manuscript of the Gospels enshrined in a Dublin library, is considered possibly the most beautiful such work in the world, it was preceded by the *Book of Kildare*. Seen as late as the 12th century by a historian whose description makes it comparable to Kells, the Kildare example disappeared during the English invasion in that same century.

Kildare began simply enough. Brigid started with her own oratory, or place of prayer, a cell built under an oak tree (*Cill-Dara*) in what had been a pagan sanctuary. (The Druid faith centered on nature worship, making temples unnecessary. This may explain the simplicity of religious architecture in Irish tradition.)

By the time Brigid invites Conleth to become a bishop and share jurisdiction with her at Kildare, the monastic village has assumed the proportions of a city. There are blacksmiths, carpenters, a granary and all else needed to be self-sufficient.

Conleth, before taking up the religious life, had been a metalworker, and this craft is added to Kildare's other artistic endeavors. The monastery produces church bells, chalices, crosiers and other liturgical objects for Ireland's burgeoning churches and monasteries.

Even with expansion, churches such as the one at Kildare continue to be built in the plain, timbered style, though interiors are hung with rich tapestries and the walls covered with frescoes. Down the center of the Kildare nave, a screen divides monks from nuns. In the daily tasks they might work side by side, but when it comes to worship, they pray separately.

In Brigid's day the monastery serves as ecclesiastical base for the Irish Church rather than the diocese, as elsewhere in Europe. As a result, power centered in the abbot and abbess instead of the bishop. (The diocesan structure was patterned after a standard unit of Roman government. Ireland, having escaped occupation by Roman legions, lacks that model. It seems logical to follow their own social order, based on tribal divisions.)

Attached to the churches of major monasteries are what become known as "cathedral schools." Many of the schools come to number nearly a thousand students, who might lodge at the monastery if room is available, or in nearby houses, free of charge. But generally they build huts for themselves in the neighborhood. Kildare's, an important school, attracts students and scholars from all parts of Europe with a curriculum encompassing the seven liberal arts as well as religious studies.

With all the activity of Kildare and her other communities, Brigid still aids the needy, though her unbounded charity at times upsets even her nuns. She also entertains a constant stream of visitors. All guests are treated alike—whether bishop, chieftain or leper. When a feast day nears, she does not find it beneath her dignity to brew ale for the occasion. Some visitors come for the hospitality, others for advice. Finian, for example, learned from Brigid how to organize a monastery before building his celebrated one at Clonard.

As Mother Abbess of all Ireland's convents, Brigid knows well how to exercise authority, for part of her background is royal, her inheritance from Dubthach. But she never forgets either what it was like to be on the low end of the social scale in the Druid's dairy. To the end of her long and healthy life, Brigid can be found milking cows, making butter and cheese and laboring in the fields, singing as she does so, for music gives her great pleasure. In the solitude of meadow, sky and fresh air she nourishes her spirit.

Many are the whimsical stories the Irish like to tell of Brigid, the classic one being the time she dried her wet cloak on a sunbeam. The searcher after her very real contributions to Christianity and the Church may grow frustrated over the recital of impossible-sounding tales. Yet in the end it becomes apparent that the poetic parable tells the most important truth about this exuberant Irish saint: Authentic holiness wears the face of joy.

AFTERWARD

Brigid's gifts to the Christian world include helping lay the foundations of education for the laity through monastery schools, which developed into the universities of the Middle Ages. Moreover, she gave the women of her country the opportunity to use their energies and intellect in a way previously not open to them. For many generations after her, Kildare would continue to be ruled by a double line of abbesses and abbot-bishops. Only in medieval times were convents placed entirely under the jurisdiction of men.

The abbesses and abbots of Brigid's era laid the foundation for Ireland's Golden Age—the centuries in which it remained a beacon of light while the continent experienced social stagnation and frequent chaos. The Irish produced a new flowering of scholars, well-rounded, intellectually tolerant, "unfettered minds," in one writer's words. At the same time they pursued the ascetic life, though they didn't talk about their heroic penances but just did them—ascetics with a smile! When Irish missionaries begin going to England, Scotland and the continent, they take along the special brand of enthusiastic piety.

Late in the eighth century, Irish monastic culture became the victim of Viking raids; monasteries were plundered and burned. Even so, until the 12th-century invasion by England and the crushing occupation which followed, Gaelic culture was regarded as one of the most advanced in Europe.

Hilda of Whitby

BACKGROUND

Not all waves of conversions occurred through the efforts of vowed missionaries. Women of royalty often played an influential role. For example, in the waning years of the fifth century, Clovis, king of the Franks, had accepted Baptism in response to the promptings of his wife, the devout Queen Clotilda. This added considerably to the domain of Christianity, since Clovis's kingdom eventually included most of territorial France as well as southwest Germany. The first Frankish ruler to convert, he set a precedent for future kings in the West by becoming a defender of Christianity. Needless to say, his nobility found it advisable to follow him to the baptistery, as eventually did most of his other subjects.

Women of royal blood set another trend: becoming nuns and founding their own religious communities. The first to do so was Radegund, another Frankish queen, around the middle of the sixth century. Forced into marriage, she managed to escape the unhappy situation and went on to establish an abbey at Poitiers in west central France. Her abbey was the original of the great double monasteries to flourish in her country.

On the opposite side of the channel, the first convent in England was founded in Folkestone in 630 by the king of Kent for his daughter Eanswythe, honored as England's first

nun. Since rebuilt, the church he erected for her—and
bearing her name—is the pride of today's Folkestone.

YORK, KINGDOM OF NORTHUMBRIA, 627

The *Anglo-Saxon Chronicle*
reports: "This year was King Edwin baptized at Easter, with
all his people, by Paulinus."

In this essentially pagan land, when the king decides to
convert to Christianity, the court as well as a number of his
subjects do likewise. The occasion comes about as a result of
the arrival two years before of Edwin's Christian bride,
Ethelberga of Kent. That kingdom, in the south of England,
had its introduction to the faith only a few decades earlier
when missionaries were sent from Rome—Paulinus among
them. (Though Christianity had reached England with the
Roman legions, it never became widespread.)

Paulinus, now bishop, performs the multiple baptisms in
the "cathedral," a small wooden church. One of his new
converts is a 13-year-old niece of the king named Hilda.
When she was just a baby, her father was banished by
another king and died of poisoning in exile. The girl has since
been reared at court. History mentions her mother only in
reference to Hilda's infancy.

These are turbulent, sometimes savage times as the
leaders of rival kingdoms in England wage war against each
other for territorial supremacy. When Edwin is killed in
battle, the Northumbrian throne falls to men who are still
pagans. The queen and her small children, with Bishop
Paulinus as escort, flee to the safety of Christian Kent, never
to return. Hilda remains, however, for her roots are in the
north.

Within a few years, the throne is regained by a genuinely
devout Christian. The new King Oswald, who had been in
exile at Iona, an island off the western coast of Scotland,
invites monks from that Irish missionary base to evangelize

his kingdom. They respond by establishing churches and schools, using as their center another island, Lindisfarne, this one not far from the king's court on the northeastern coast of England.

When Oswald is killed in battle, fighting over the throne resumes. The constant strife may explain why Hilda, now 33 and feeling the call to be a nun, decides to join her sister in a convent near Paris. Of noble birth and well-educated, Hilda might have married had there been parents to arrange it. Perhaps she feels lucky simply not to have been carried off as part of the spoils of war, as so often happened to women then.

In 647 she travels down to East Anglia, where her widowed sister's son is king, and stays at his court while awaiting passage to France. During her prolonged wait for a ship, the Irish missionary Bishop Aidan arrives in East Anglia to seek her assistance. He wants to resume his work in Northumbria which was interrupted by the fighting. With the situation calm once more, he persuades her to return.

His idea is that Hilda help him develop the monastic life according to the Irish approach: combining scholarship with holiness. He gives her a small piece of land by the River Wear, where she and a few friends of similar inclination take up residence, spending a quiet year in prayer. The end of that period coincides with the departure of the founder-abbess of Hartlepool, on the North Sea coast. That abbess had been the first nun in Northumbria, consecrated about 640 by Bishop Aidan.

As new abbess of the Hartlepool convent, Hilda perfects the methods of organization and discipline that will prepare her for the important work in her future. Even now she earns the high regard of Aidan and other men of religion.

The story of her eight years at Hartlepool is recounted in Bede's *Ecclesiatical History of the English People*. Bede, a monk born in 643, spent all his life in Northumbria and knew some of Hilda's contemporaries. The monk writes of her "innate wisdom, and her delight in the service of God," reporting that all ask for her advice, "not only ordinary people but even kings and princes." Hilda directs her nuns in a life marked by "strict observance of justice, piety, and chastity, and of the other virtues, but mostly of peace and charity...."

Oswy, the current king, wins a decisive victory over the pagan leader of a rival kingdom. Having vowed to consecrate his baby daughter Elfleda to God in return for victory, he entrusts her to Hilda's care. With the baby goes a dowry of sorts: "12 estates." The extensive piece of property apparently includes the site known then by the Old English name *Streaneshalch* (translated "Lighthouse Bay"), but more familiar to history by its later name: Whitby.

In 657 Hilda supervises the building at Whitby of a double monastery to house monks and nuns—a common arrangement for early English monasteries. The setting, about 30 miles down the coast from Hartlepool, is unusually dramatic: on a headland 300 feet above the bay, where the River Esk empties into the North Sea. From the commanding hilltop can be seen the surrounding moors as well as the ocean.

The complex of buildings making up a convent for nuns and an abbey for monks are of austerely plain construction, similar to the monastic settlements of Ireland. (Hilda's mentor, Aidan, has since died, to be succeeded by another Irishman, Finan.)

With the completion of the monastery, the nuns and monks elect Hilda their superior. Under her direction, Whitby becomes famous as a center of holiness and scholarship. Like the communities of primitive Christianity, the monks and nuns hold all goods in common, with no separation of classes into rich and poor. (Monasteries on the continent cannot always make this claim.) The hundreds of religious who come under Hilda's supervision spend countless hours studying, copying by hand the Bible and other great books, translating and illuminating manuscripts. In fact, the Whitby library becomes known as one of England's finest.

The abbess also attaches a school to the complex which attracts scholars from other countries. As Bede observed: "All who desired to be instructed in sacred reading had masters at hand to teach them." Music has a role in the

cultured atmosphere, too, and almost everyone in the
monastery can play the harp or other instrument.

Hilda's spiritual and intellectual guidance eventually
results in five of her monks being raised to the episcopacy,
and Whitby's reputation is such that bishops look to it as
their source for clergymen.

The indefatigable abbess also attends to the welfare of lay
persons living in the area overseen by her monastery (for
abbesses of Hilda's rank maintained a major say in the
administration of wide territories). On the grounds itself is a
house for the sick.

Looked on as the most learned woman in England of her
time, she appears to enjoy most nurturing or fostering the
gifts of others, whether it be the training of future bishops or
future poets. Again from Bede: "All that knew her called her
mother."

One day Hilda happens to hear that an illiterate cowherd
employed at Whitby shows an unusual talent for song. She
calls Caedmon in, recognizes his poetic ability, persuades
him to leave the tending of cows to others and invites him to
join the religious community. Given instruction in Scripture,
Caedmon composes songs in the vernacular, using words
easily memorized in order to make stories of their faith
understandable and interesting for the common people—a
need Hilda clearly recognizes. For example, he describes
creation in this verse:

> "First, for a roof,
> O'er the children of earth,
> He established the heavens,
> And founded the world,
> And spread the dry land
> For the living to dwell in.
> Lord Everlasting!
> Almighty God!"

Ultimately, Caedmon achieves fame as England's first
Christian poet.

An age when both the northern and southern kingdoms
are primarily Christian ought to be peaceful. For when King

Oswy defeated his pagan adversary, it meant the collapse of the last pagan stronghold—one that had occupied the heartland of England. In a sense though, the pagan section so strategically located had served as a sort of buffer between the Celtic- or Irish-oriented Church of the north and the Rome-dominated Church of the south.

The two differed chiefly in this respect: A Roman-style institution emphasized a hierarchical structure and strict conformance in thought and ritual, while the Irish favored a free-spirited approach which resulted in independence of thought and a lack of centralization. The inevitable clash will come about over a seemingly trivial matter.

King Oswy is accustomed to the Celtic tradition brought and sustained by dedicated Irish missionaries. But his wife Eanfleda is from Kent, the kingdom converted by missionaries from Rome. Though nothing so serious as doctrinal differences exist, practices vary. Chief among them is the date Easter is celebrated.

A century or two earlier, Rome had revised the system of determining the date, but the Celtic Church stayed with the old way. Things came to a head: "When the king was breaking his fast and solemnizing the Lord's Easter, then the queen and her company continued yet the fast and kept the day of palms." This put the entire court in a quandary, uncertain which of the royal couple to follow.

On a lesser scale but of concern to the monks is the tonsure, the direction in which their heads were shaved. The Celts shaved the front of the head from ear to ear, leaving the hair on the back of the head to grow long. With the Roman tonsure, all hair is shaved except for a ring encircling the head. The younger monks grow increasingly resentful over the difference.

These somewhat mild issues mask the underlying one: Which party will prevail—Celtic or Roman? The future of the English Church depended on the outcome. To resolve the impasse, a synod is called in 664 and Whitby, because of its prestige, is chosen as the meeting place under the presidency of its abbess.

An abbot from each side presents his case before the king,

who sits as judge. Oswy's natural sympathy favors the Celtic cause, but as he listens, he is won over by the argument that Rome has inherited the keys of the kingdom directly from Peter. That's enough for Oswy. He cannot, will not contradict Peter.

Hilda too leans toward the Irish side, for her mentors were from that background, but she yields for the sake of peace. Harmony in the English Church (with a few exceptions) is preserved, and the unity of Western Christendom strengthened.

Hilda goes on governing the monastery even though, in her last seven years, she suffers from ill health. Ever a lover of peace, in her final words to the community "she urged them to maintain the gospel peace among themselves and with others."

AFTERWARD

The king's baby daughter Elfleda, who had been entrusted to Hilda's care, grew up to become Hilda's successor as head of Whitby. Women played a prominent role in Anglo-Saxon society, including participation in the intellectual renaissance that began in Hilda's time.

The tradition developed in English monasteries and the schools associated with them was characterized by discipline, a sense of stability and a high standard of scholarship. Many religious centers became famous for their learning.

Long before becoming one politically, England achieved religious unity, thanks to the Whitby synod. This brought its Church into closer contact with the Church on the continent. Bridging the two would have enormous impact in the following century, when English missionaries took their monastic tradition abroad. This included a passion for learning inherited from the Irish and organizational skills

which came to them by way of Rome—a combination of
qualities which practically ensure success in mission lands.
As an added bonus, England provided Charlemagne with an
outstanding scholar to direct his palace school: Alcuin, a
Northumbrian-educated monk, who helped spark the
Carolingian Renaissance.

Lioba, Anglo-Saxon Missionary to Germany

BACKGROUND

In the first decade or so of the
eighth century, the once-flourishing Church in North Africa
was overrun by Muslims. The faithful in Egypt soon became
a minority, while the armies of Islam embarked on the
conquest of Spain. Their advance into Europe was not halted
until a defeat by Charles Martel (grandfather of
Charlemagne) at Poitiers in 732.

At the eastern end of the Mediterranean, though
Constantinople was so far spared, the constant threat of
Islam affected policies. At various times Byzantine emperors
used the issue of iconoclasm (image-breaking) to assert their
authority over both Church and State. This controversy in
the East over using religious statues and pictures—some
called it idolatry—often erupted into violence not unlike that
which occurred earlier with regard to the doctrine on the
nature of Christ.

Along with many monks, women were especially
prominent in the defense of icons. They had the support of
the Church in Rome. (Taking sides was to create enemies in
the East for Rome.)

Life was more peaceable in England, at least in monastic
enclaves such as the one founded in 718 by Cuthburg, sister

to a king. Her abbey at Wimborne in Wessex (the West
Country) was free to grow and prosper in relative security.
Even when Vikings began attacking England late in that
century, the eastern coast bore the brunt.

MAINZ, GERMANY, 748

In a letter to Tetta, abbess of
the great English abbey at Wimborne, Boniface asks for
assistance with his missionary work among the Frankish
tribes of Germany. He specifically requests that his younger
cousin Lioba be one of the nuns sent.

The two cousins had begun corresponding some time
before that, starting with a letter written by Lioba, then a
novice at the abbey in the southwest of England. Enclosing a
gift of Latin verses, Lioba asked for his critical opinion of her
writing. "I am longing for your help," she explained, adding
the hope "that you may not forget me while you are far
away."

Touched by what Lioba wrote, Boniface saved the letter
and began the regular exchange which deepens their
friendship in the ensuing years.

Boniface communicated with many people in England,
and from them he heard praise for Lioba's learning and
holiness, her willingness to do manual labor and her blithe
young spirit. Surely she is missionary material. Still, he must
also have had great confidence in her potential to survive in
the heathen, primitive society of Germany—particularly in
light of Lioba's sheltered and cultured background.

Born in Wessex of middle-aged parents whose hope for a
baby was almost gone, she was so cherished they called her
Lioba, meaning "the loved one." Wanting the best for their
only child, they placed her in a monastery school, since it
provided the best education for girls as well as boys. Upon
coming of age, she decided to become a nun, a choice which
in this instance entailed perpetual enclosure, with travel

outside permitted under special circumstances. (Wimborne was a double monastery where Abbess Tetta ruled over both nuns and monks. There was no contact between members of the two communities, however.)

When Boniface sends for Lioba, she has become the novice mistress and one of the more promising members at Wimborne. Reluctantly, the abbess lets her go, along with a small band of other nuns, to set up a convent in the heartland of Germany.

Boniface knows full well the conditions the women must face, though the situation has improved since papal commission first made him apostle to Germany. True, the Church existed in this wilderness land prior to his arrival, but he found it in a pitiable state. Christian ritual mingled freely with pagan practices. Magic spells were common to all, and so was nature worship. Boniface had been appalled, as he wrote to Pope Zacharias in 742, to discover that deacons "have spent their lives since childhood in debauchery, adultery and every kind of uncleanness...and who even now, when they have four or five or even more concubines in their beds at night, are brazen enough to call themselves deacons and read out the Gospel." Even worse, Boniface went on, they continued this life-style even after becoming priests. Church reform was desperately needed.

He could not begin to think then of setting up religious communities of women. Now, after he has labored more than two decades to bring order, the time seems right.

Lioba and her companions arrive at Mainz after a fatiguing journey, first crossing the English Channel, then making their way by road and river to the monastery Boniface has ready for them. It is called Bischofsheim, or Bishop's House, which suggests that he is turning over his own residence to the women.

He greets them warmly, especially pleased to meet his cousin Lioba—the one described as having "a face like an angel and always pleasant." He puts her in charge of the fledgling community, and this she will govern as abbess for the next 28 years, though she also establishes elsewhere in Germany houses over which Boniface gives her authority.

The nuns are to follow the Benedictine Rule, as do Boniface's monks: combining manual labor with intellectual pursuits and observing moderation in all things rather than severe asceticism. Life in this wilderness land can be rough enough.

Boniface's aim for both nuns and monks is that they work to set up monasteries throughout the land—Christian centers to provide a civilizing influence. In the past, many in the Frankish kingdom converted out of loyalty to tribal chiefs. The net result was faith of only a superficial nature. To sink deep roots, religious education is called for; in the process, vocations can be drawn from the native population to ensure the future of the Church.

Lioba's nuns assume charge of educating Frankish girls. Their convent setting is a far cry from that of Wimborne Abbey, but wherever a colony of religious settle, the surrounding countryside undergoes a transformation. Clearing land for the planting of crops has the most visible effect. Additionally, no matter how makeshift the monastery buildings at first, the presence of holy men and women serves as a powerful antidote to the dark forces of paganism, which still maintain a stronghold. Even human sacrifice occasionally occurs.

Typically, settlements of all kinds, whether secular or religious, are built on Germany's abundant waterways, for these prove by far the safest way to travel. Between the population centers come wide stretches of uncultivated forests without roads or, at best, with poorly marked ones. Brigands as well as wild animals pose dangers there.

Lioba and her nuns do more than teach, for every monastic settlement is also a place of refuge for the sick or hungry and a hospice for the traveler. Anyone who knocks at the door, even a criminal, must be welcomed and cared for. Because Frankish rulers provide no welfare for the needy, the Church acts as protector. And the population suffers hardships aplenty: epidemics among livestock, plagues among people, famine, endless winters, floods. There is no technology to ease the problems of uncertain climate or disease—only the selfless efforts of nuns and monks.

In the face of all this, Lioba gives ample evidence of being a reassuring presence to the superstitious peasants. Her unperturbable calm becomes the stuff of legends. There is the time, for instance, that a fire breaks out in a nearby village, spreading rapidly from one thatched roof to the next. The fire grows to threaten even the monastery. In panic, the villagers rush to find the abbess. In her quiet yet practical way, Lioba directs them to take buckets from the river that flows past and throw water on the flames. When they follow her order, the flames are extinguished. "At this miracle," reports a monk named Rudolf, "the whole crowd stood amazed and broke out into the praise of God, who through the faith and prayers of his handmaid had delivered them so extraordinarily from a terrible danger." (To Rudolf is owed the biography of Lioba, based on information he obtained from her contemporaries.)

On another occasion, during a fierce thunderstorm, the terror-stricken villagers take refuge in the church. Lioba invites them to pray with her, but they are too overcome with fear. As the storm continues unabated, she opens the church doors and "stretches out her hands to heaven and three times invokes the mercy of Christ," asking that "he would come quickly to the help of his people." Suddenly the storm dies away and the sun comes out.

Almost as fabled as her courage is Lioba's hospitality. According to Rudolf, "She kept open house for all without exception, and even when she was fasting gave banquets and washed the feet of the guests with her own hands, at once the guardian and the minister of the practice instituted by our Lord."

Most days are spent more routinely, however, with the nuns dividing their days into prayer, study, teaching and manual work. The work may be in the bakehouse, the brewhouse or in performing household duties. A particular sphere of activity is the production of books. The scriptorium keeps busy copying manuscripts to use in the training of future clergy and nuns.

Lioba is never without a book herself, continuing her own studies though already well-versed in the Old and New

Testaments, the writings of the Church Fathers and canon law. Neither are the liberal arts neglected. When the abbess lies down for the midday rest, the younger nuns take turns reading to her from Scripture. But even when she appears to be almost asleep, they dare not skip a word or she will immediately make a correction.

She encourages her nuns in scholarship. For example, Huneberc, an Anglo-Saxon nun at their convent in Heidenheim, writes an account of the monk Willibald's travels. (The two missionaries are good friends.) It is the only narrative in existence of an eighth-century pilgrimage to the Holy Land and also the earliest travel book by an English writer.

The women obviously regard their superior with great affection. The small cup from which the abstemious Lioba drinks is known as "the Beloved's little one." And to Boniface she is the "dear one," for as they work closely together, the bonds of friendship grow stronger.

When he prepares to leave for the dangerous mission field of Frisia (part of the Netherlands) to preach to its pagans, perhaps he has a premonition of the martyrdom which awaits him there, for he asks Lioba to meet him at his headquarters in Mainz prior to departure. Maybe Boniface recalls his cousin's earlier gift of Latin verses that he might not forget her while far away. As a parting gift—to remember him by—he presents his "dear one" with his monk's cowl.

Then, calling together his senior monks, Boniface reaffirms a wish made previously: that after death, he and Lioba should be laid to rest in the same tomb at Fulda, his favorite monastery. He explains why: "that we who in this life together have served Christ with the same devotion and love, may together await the day of resurrection."

In the long years following Boniface's martyrdom in Frisia, Lioba, though admittedly lonely, continues the apostolic work the two once shared. Her closest friend during this latter stage of her life is Hildegard, wife of Charlemagne (who in 771 became sole ruler of the Franks). Much as Lioba dislikes the hectic atmosphere of the royal court at Aachen, for the sake of their friendship she sometimes will accept Hildegard's insistent invitations. There, Rudolf writes, "the princes loved her, the nobles received her, the bishops welcomed her with joy. And because of her wide knowledge of the Scriptures and her prudence in counsel they often discussed spiritual matters and ecclesiastical discipline with her."

At other times Lioba visits the various convents around Germany to monitor their progress. What she likes best, though, is going to Fulda to pray at the tomb of Boniface—a privilege denied all other women, for entrance to the monastery is forbidden to them. (Boniface in his lifetime had granted her the favor of praying at Fulda.)

In the final years, Lioba retires to a small convent four miles south of Mainz, where she spends her days in fasting and prayer. Upon her death in 780, the monks at Fulda decide against carrying out Boniface's last request, seeing it somehow as an impropriety. They elect instead to bury her at Fulda, but in a tomb apart from her cousin's.

AFTERWARD

History regards the missionary endeavors of Boniface, Lioba and company in Germany as "the most important apostolic work of the eighth century." The immediate results were beneficial enough: a civilizing effect on a primitive society and education as a weapon in the struggle to survive a hostile environment. Wherever religious settlements were founded, monks and nuns cleared and cultivated the surrounding wilderness and passed on more advanced agricultural techniques to their German neighbors.

Through their promotion of learning and the arts, monks and nuns helped lay the groundwork for the Carolingian Renaissance. Some say the spread of monasteries had a more lasting impact on Europe than Charlemagne's empire-building. (Boniface's and Lioba's way of evangelizing was in marked contrast to Charlemagne's, who was inclined to make wholesale conversions at the point of a sword.)

In the long term, bringing Christian civilization to the heartland of Europe was crucial to the continent's historical development. As the various Frankish tribes united in a common religion, the Holy Roman Empire emerged. In that empire, too, several centuries later, the convents Lioba established would play a role, still bearing fruit as a new renaissance came about.

Ludmila of Bohemia

BACKGROUND

The Carolingian dynasty, founded in the seventh century, reached its zenith when Charlemagne was crowned emperor of the West by Pope Leo III on Christmas Day, 800. On the throne in the East, the Empress Irene not only disliked the idea of a rival power, but also scoffed at that "barbarian" from a Frankish tribe brazen enough to seek such an honored position. (She sat on the throne at Constantinople as a result of having first discredited the heir, her son, then having him blinded.)

Neither the Carolingians nor the Byzantines could measure up to the two magnificent civilizations contemporary with their times. In China the T'ang dynasty was creating a dazzling array of works of art, poetry and scientific developments such as the printing press (which was not seen in Europe until centuries later). And in Baghdad, the Abbasid dynasty reflected Arab achievements of like brilliance in an empire stretching from the borders of India to the Iberian Peninsula.

Though unheralded, in a remote corner of Europe there quietly sprang up a dynasty destined to add luster to the honor roll of saints. As tradition tells it, a Bohemian queen, Libussa, married a peasant named Premysl at an unknown date in the eighth century. The marriage gave birth to the Premyslide dynasty, which eventually united the Slavic settlements of Bohemia into a single duchy.

DUCHY OF BOHEMIA, c. 880

The first Christians to be converted in their land, Duke Borivoj and his wife Ludmila (daughter of a Slav prince), show enthusiasm for their new faith by building Bohemia's first church at the site of the royal residence north of Prague. They dedicate it to St. Clement, an esteemed pope and martyr of the first century.

As ruler of the duchy (part of today's Czechoslovakia), Borivoj attempts to impose Christianity on the pagan population but meets with stiff resistance, particularly from the leading families and the pagan priests. The latter's power is extensive enough to control the justice system, administering the laws of the land. Though in its primitive form the Slavic religion revolves around vague spirits of nature, where life is more developed (as in Prague), there are deities representing the forces of good and evil, temples and a hierarchy of priests.

While it may be common practice for monarchs to enforce their own religious beliefs on the people, in this case the opposition proves too strong. When an uprising begins, Borivoj and Ludmila flee east to the court of the Moravian prince for protection until order can be restored.

Order returns only after the leader of the rebellion is killed. Home again, the royal couple build their next church on Castle Hill in Prague near an old heathen place of sacrifice and dedicate it to the Virgin Mary. But they otherwise tread more slowly in conversion attempts, for the native religion remains thoroughly entrenched. (Although in 845, German missionaries in the wider region had baptized 14 princes and their households—the earliest recorded baptisms in Czech history—nothing further seems to have come of that episode.)

The next set of missionaries to Slavic lands (Slav tribes

inhabited much of eastern Europe) would come by invitation of the Moravian kingdom, Bohemia's neighbor to the east. Because only a short time has elapsed since Moravia won back independence from Charlemagne's heirs, the prince fears German missionaries would have too much influence. Wanting Christianity for his kingdom but not Germanic rule again, he asks the Byzantine emperor at Constantinople to dispatch missionaries from the eastern half of the Church. (The formal break between the patriarch at Constantinople and the pope at Rome has yet to come, though the rivalry is heating up.)

Two monks, Cyril and Methodius, accept the invitation and meet with immediate success in Moravia, for the two, having mastered the Slavic language, preach and conduct the liturgy in the vernacular. When the pope learns of this, he summons the monks to Rome, hears their case, then gives permission to continue use of the Slavic language at Mass. Cyril's death occurs in 869, while Methodius, responsible for baptizing Borivoj and Ludmila, dies in 884.

These are turbulent times everywhere in Europe. Charlemagne's successors are battling over who is to rule which territory; the Magyars, a tribe out of Asia, conduct a roving war on horseback; Vikings and Saracens invade different parts of the continent; and the papacy is in a vastly weakened condition. (About the time of Ludmila's baptism, the only strong pope of the ninth century was hammered to death by his own relatives.)

In the meantime, Ludmila gives birth to two sons, while Borivoj is occupied with political struggles. Despite Bohemia's geographical location as a frontier land, its major town, Prague, is far from a backwater in commercial terms. The castle, in fact, is a fortification which protects Prague's growing position as a trade center. Its greatest asset is the Moldau River, which flows the entire length of the country, connecting in the north with a German waterway. In consequence, Prague serves as crossroads for the lucrative European routes, both north-south and east-west.

When Borivoj dies in 895 at the age of 35, his two sons, barely of age to govern, succeed him as joint rulers. Their mother remains in the background, quietly but steadfastly working in behalf of Christianity.

When the first grandson is born, her son Ratislav and daughter-in-law Drahomira entrust Ludmila with the child's upbringing. Her chaplain, Paul of Ancona, who had been a personal disciple of Methodius, baptizes the baby Wenceslaus and later helps with the boy's education. He and Ludmila, of considerable learning herself, teach Wenceslaus to read Latin as well as Slavic and train him to abide by the highest moral principles.

When Wenceslaus's father dies while fighting the Magyars (Ludmila's other son was killed earlier), the forceful and ambitious Drahomira assumes the regency, for her son has not yet attained his majority. Until now Christianity has been making slow gains, but Drahomira, who is no more than a nominal believer, becomes a willing tool of the anti-Christian party. The nobility belonging to it encourage her jealousy of Ludmila's influence on Wenceslaus, and Drahomira promptly removes the young man from his grandmother's care. Only in secret will he be able to worship or to see his Christian friends.

The new regent also issues in strictest terms an order forbidding priests and others who profess Christianity to instruct children. She removes Christian magistrates installed previously by either Duke Borivoj or one of his sons and replaces them with followers of paganism. Drahomira suspects—true or not—that her mother-in-law may be trying to persuade Wenceslaus to take the reins of government before he comes of ruling age. The popular young man could rally the citizenry to his side and thus save the faith. Ludmila herself, because of an inherent gentleness and charity, is greatly loved by the Bohemian people. (Interestingly, Ludmila's name in Slavic means "people's love.")

Drahomira's suspicions are further fed by tales concocted by the anti-Christian faction. Though no one knows for certain if the regent had any role in the murder plot, two nobles of the pagan party go to the Castle of Tetin outside of Prague, where Ludmila is spending her "retirement." There, on September 16, 921, they strangle her while she is at prayer in the chapel. She thus becomes Bohemia's first martyr.

AFTERWARD

Shortly after, Drahomira, in political maneuvering to aid enemies of the German king, gets into trouble and is banished from the court. Wenceslaus is proclaimed ruler. He negotiates peace with the invading Germans, initiating a policy of friendly relations with them, then strives to strengthen Christianity in his kingdom. Neither policy sits well with the opposition among the nobility, especially the non-Christians. They work constantly to undermine Wenceslaus.

Of a spiritual bent, he thinks of abdicating in favor of his younger brother, Boleslav, and going into a monastery, but reconsiders. He begins the building of the great Church of St. Vitus in Prague; in tribute to his grandmother he has her body brought from its grave in a Tetin church to be buried in the Church of St. George, built by his father. Despite frequent and sometimes violent opposition to Christianity, churches have continued to be erected in order to serve the steadily increasing number of faithful.

Trying to rule with both justice and mercy, guided by the principles his grandmother taught him, Wenceslaus recalls Drahomira to the court—her days of intrigue over. She has no part in the ensuing conspiracy, but Wenceslaus's brother does. In 929, having allied himself with the opposition when he believes his chance of succession to the throne is all but over (for a son is born to Wenceslaus), Boleslav, with three other men, intercepts Wenceslaus as he makes his way to Mass through a private passage from the castle. Boleslav comes at him with a sword.

As Wenceslaus lies dying at the church door, he says to Boleslav, "Brother, may God forgive you."

Like Ludmila, Wenceslaus too was immediately

proclaimed a martyr. But Boleslav, having seized power, drove out the priests and persecuted Christians. His own mother and sister fled for safety, not knowing what he might do next. Eventually Otto the Great of Germany took steps forcing Boleslav to restore the faith, and the latter even accepted Baptism before his death. His son, called Boleslav the Good, inspired by the memory of a saintly grandmother and uncle, succeeded in making all of Bohemia Christian.

Conversions were especially important to the Church during this period because declining numbers resulted from chaotic conditions everywhere. The eastern Mediterranean lands and North Africa, containing much of the wealth of the Church in terms of people, material goods and treasured shrines, had been lost to Islam in the two preceding centuries.

In an age when there was little for the Church to cheer about (no pope emerged to give inspired leadership and even saints of note were rare), Ludmila's role as holy woman and promoter of Christianity became all the more valuable. She deservedly gets credit for a significant contribution in spreading the civilizing light of faith, extending its boundaries east.

Our century adds a footnote to her story: During the "Prague Spring" in 1968, the city's Wenceslaus Square served as rallying point for the country's unsuccessful but courageous uprising against Communist rule. The longing for freedom could not be crushed, however. In 1989 the people of Prague gathered once more at the Square, this time accomplishing their goal in a remarkably peaceful revolution. Wenceslaus and Ludmila continue to be venerated and emulated by their people.

Adelaide, Empress of the Holy Roman Empire

BACKGROUND

As the 10th century dawned, the great population shifts on the continent were finally coming to an end. One indication of this was that a group of Danish Vikings put down roots half a century earlier on the Irish coast. Their settlement developed into Dublin.

In 911, another settlement of significance took place on the northwest coast of France when the French king bribed a tribe of Vikings with the offer of territory. He managed to convince the Norsemen (hence *Normans, Normandy*) that a steady income from commerce would profit them more in the long run than piracy.

The combination of invasions and migrations had been a severe hindrance to Europe's progress. Christianity had been hit especially hard by the destruction of monastic culture when Vikings plundered and burned monasteries—not to mention the losses to Islam.

Recovery was in store, however. Just a year prior to the Normandy settlement, an even greater harbinger of happier times occurred in eastern France, in the region of Burgundy: the founding of a monastery called Cluny. It would be a name forever identified with Church reform and spiritual revival.

In their darkest ages Europeans had been helpless. No leader strong enough to cope had emerged after Charlemagne's death. There was a vacuum in the Church, too, for no pope of moral stature or political clout had materialized either. In 936 that changed with the ascension to the German throne of Otto I, destined to become Otto the Great.

PAVIA, NORTHERN ITALY, CHRISTMAS DAY, 951

Otto I, king of Germany, marries Adelaide, 20-year-old widow of the king of Lombardy. The wedding marks a happy ending to some trying and even frightening times for the young queen.

Her first husband was poisoned during a political struggle over control of Lombardy (northern Italy). Berengar, the man responsible for the poisoning, then tried to force Adelaide to marry his son. When she refused, Berengar imprisoned her in a castle near Lake Garda where, over a four-month period, she endured rough treatment.

Adelaide had loyal friends, however, and one of them, a priest, rescued her by digging a subterranean passage through which she made her escape. Hiding in the woods, they survived on fish from the lake until asylum could be arranged at a castle on Church property.

As all this was going on, Otto, the powerful German king, marched south to straighten out the troubles in Lombardy, a move which promised to strengthen his own position. Once in Italy, he met Adelaide (described as "a marvel of grace and beauty" by her biographer, Odilo, abbot of Cluny, who knew her personally). Otto surely made an impression too, for he was a giant of a man with a ruddy complexion and long red beard.

On his part, their marriage is politically wise, for Adelaide still bears a claim to the throne of Lombardy. Moreover, she is the daughter of the late Rudolf II of

Burgundy, a small but strategically located kingdom in eastern France, and her mother comes from Swabia in southern Germany. But beyond that—and despite an almost 20-year difference in age—the two fall in love.

Upon their return to Germany, Adelaide wins the affection of its people just as she had the Lombards'. In every important undertaking of government, she can be found at Otto's side; in a rare action, he has her image stamped on the reverse half of German coins.

He dreams of restoring the old Roman empire, making it the Holy Roman Empire, God's kingdom on earth. But for all the politicking involved in that, Otto is a man of exemplary moral behavior. Those who work with the king dub him Otto the Pious.

Adelaide perceives as her special province bringing her influence to bear in matters of culture and religion. (The two are customarily intertwined.) On the cultural side, she and the ladies of the court create an atmosphere of learning through their encouragement and support of literature and the fine arts. Germany is just becoming the most prosperous country in Europe, and times are right for the high level of artistic achievement which history terms the Ottonian Renaissance.

Craftsmen produce exquisite work in gold filigree and ivory. One ivory book cover, for example, depicts in detail the celebration of the Mass. Convents enjoy a reputation as literary centers. At the convent of Gandersheim in Saxony, a nun named Hroswitha writes plays in classic Latin which are comparable in style to the Roman playwright Terence, though much different in content. (Hroswitha's writings are being rediscovered by today's literary world.) Royal support also goes to monastic schools that are more like colleges and boast well-stocked libraries.

Adelaide knows how to promote spiritual enterprises too. She presents abbots at court, and through her intercession many monasteries are founded or expanded. In fact, her generosity toward churches and monasteries is thought to be excessive, although no one voices a criticism aloud while Otto is alive.

Both Adelaide and Otto take particular interest in sending missionaries to the Slavic people who border Germany on the northeast, aiming to draw them into the rest of Christendom. Until that happens, the Slavs will constitute a threat. Another threat—this one to all of Europe—are the Magyars. When Otto defeats them in a brilliant victory in 955, he earns the title "the Great." He compels the roving warriors to settle in the territory later known as Hungary.

In 962 he and Adelaide journey to Rome to be crowned by the pope as emperor and empress of the Holy Roman Empire. Her old enemy, Berengar, is again stirring up trouble, this time in league with the pope. Otto had given the man a second chance during the Lombardy business, but further intrigues he will not allow. During subsequent imprisonment in Germany, Berengar dies and Adelaide takes in his young daughter, educating her to become one of the ladies at court. (Of Adelaide's own daughters one, Emma, from her first husband, marries the king of France; two of the three daughters she and Otto have profess as nuns.)

At the age of 42, Adelaide becomes a widow for the second time when Otto dies while attending vespers at the Cathedral of Magdeburg. Prior to that, he had arranged, with the cooperation of the Byzantine Emperor, for marriage between his son Otto and a Greek princess. Succeeding his father in 973, the 19-year-old Otto II appears at first to be a ruler in the same mold, but soon makes a move toward independence from the past. His wife Theophano supports him and finds allies among the courtiers who had objected privately in the past to Adelaide's generosity to the Church. When the situation threatens to turn into open conflict, the peace-loving Adelaide departs Germany, going to stay with her brother Conrad at his court in Burgundy.

Nothing could be more natural than that she take an interest now in conditions of the French Church. In addition to giving aid to abbeys, she sees to the rebuilding of the Monastery of St. Martin of Tours, which had been destroyed by fire. (Its shrine in honor of the saint is high on the list of Europe's important places of pilgrimage.)

Church rebuilding of another sort is going on in the countryside of her native Burgundy where, early in the century, the monastery at Cluny had been founded. Because of its abbots' holiness, it becomes the center of a movement for ecclesiastical reform—badly needed in the Church but not forthcoming from Rome. The papacy in the 10th century has sunk to its lowest point in all of history, so that spiritual direction from that quarter is nonexistent. The Lateran Palace is better known for its orgies, and control of the daily papal business is in the hands of leading Roman families whose morals are absolutely appalling. Otto the Great had worked to correct the pontifical mess through political means. Cluny, on its part, starts with reform of monasteries, calling them back to New Testament values and practices. The movement grows to encompass the whole of Christendom.

In her association with Cluny, Adelaide tells the abbot, Mayeul, about the breach between her and her son Otto. She has prayed long and offered numerous sacrifices in hope of reconciliation. When she appeals to Mayeul to mediate, he manages so successfully that a repentant Otto recalls his mother to court.

In thanksgiving, she sends a messenger loaded with gifts to the shrine at Tours. Among the gifts is Otto's finest cloak, accompanied by a prayer to St. Martin: "Receive these humble presents of Adelaide, servant of the servants of God, sinner by her nature, empress by divine grace. Receive also this cloak of Otto, her only son. And pray for him, thou who hadst the glory of covering with thine own cloak our Lord, in the person of a beggar." (In the story of St. Martin's life, the cloak represents heroic charity.)

On her return to court, Otto shows a willingness to listen to his mother's advice on reforms needed in government. On one occasion, when she expresses the wish that Mayeul be named pope (the incumbent has been murdered), Otto offers the abbot the papacy, but Mayeul says he's not interested. (The Holy Roman Emperor's approval is part of the selection process.)

In 982, while fighting the Saracens (as Arab Muslims

were then called) in southern Italy, Otto suffers a disastrous defeat. The following year, he appoints his mother viceroy of Lombardy. (It is common for the German monarch to name women to leading positions in government.) That same year he again heads for southern Italy, planning this time to seek a win against the Saracens. Stopping in Rome to plan the campaign, Otto contracts a fatal case of malaria.

His premature death while still in his 20s brings on a crisis for the empire. On the northern and eastern borders, enemies from without threaten. Within, a violent struggle erupts over the question of who will assume the regency, since Otto III is just three years old.

Although Adelaide and her daughter-in-law Theophano both qualify as legitimate rulers, the two are so different in nature and outlook that joint rule seems impossible. To ensure the peace, Adelaide returns to her position in Pavia as viceroy of Lombardy. The Lombards revere their former queen and, with this in her favor, she succeeds in keeping the strategic territory loyal to the empire.

Theophano cannot bear to see her mother-in-law prospering. During the next few years, Theophano continually tries to undercut Adelaide's high standing. In 991 Theophano makes the curious remark that if she lives another full year, she will manage to oust Adelaide as viceroy. But before year's end, while on a trip through western Germany, Theophano unexpectedly dies.

This time there is no question that Adelaide will take over as regent of the empire until her grandson comes of age in 995. For guidance, she relies on Willigis, Archbishop of Mainz, who helped end the crisis when Otto II died, and on her spiritual director, Odilo, a young monk at Cluny destined soon to be its abbot. Adelaide typically shows no ill will toward those courtiers who earlier had sided with Theophano.

When Otto III reaches his majority, the 64-year-old empress gladly retires from administering the vast empire. In her new freedom, Adelaide can devote full time to prayer and the foundation and restoration of houses for monks and nuns.

Still engaged in peacemaking, too, she is en route to Burgundy in December 999, to effect a reconciliation between her nephew, the king and his rebellious subjects when she falls ill and stops at Selz, a monastery on the Rhine which she had founded. With Adelaide at the end is Odilo, now abbot of Cluny, who observes in her biography that despite her lofty position as empress, Adelaide never forgot that there is only one Lord. But perhaps the most telling assessment of her character is the remark often made of her that "she never forgot a kindness, nor ever remembered an injury."

AFTERWARD

From the middle of the 10th century to the start of the 11th, Germany took the lead in Europe, both politically and artistically. For the fresh surge of creativity known as the Ottonian Renaissance, historians credit the imperial court where Adelaide presided over matters of culture as well as religion. The artistic achievements of this renaissance set the tone for art all through the Middle Ages.

In her close association with both the aesthetic realm and spiritual reform, Adelaide played a critical role in shaping the Christian culture of Western Europe. Her friend Odilo of Cluny, by the way, is considered the greatest among all its great abbots of this period. One guesses he shared Adelaide's love of peace, for Cluny took the lead in attempting to restrict the incessant warfare among feudal lords which caught peasants in the middle with predictable devastation. An idea surfacing in 990 eventually resulted in the "Truce of God," whereby fighting was suspended every Friday, Saturday and Sunday. Later Lent was added to the "closed season."

Missionaries who had been sent to convert the Slavs living on Germany's northeastern border (the area comprising Poland) were overwhelmingly successful. In the 11th century Poland could be called thoroughly Christian.

In 999 Adelaide's grandson Otto III had his former tutor, a scholarly and devout man, named pope. Sylvester II's papacy would herald a revival of the Christian spirit where it was most urgently needed—in the papacy itself. In the following century new laws for selecting a pope would begin the process of eliminating outside interference.

Adelaide's death came just two weeks before the start of the year 1000. The approach of the millennium brought with it a pervasive mood of fear among the common people that the end of the world was in sight. When the date passed without the earth disintegrating in a vast conflagration, the universal sigh of relief was followed by a burst of energy and enthusiasm in all things religious and secular.

Margaret of Scotland

BACKGROUND

After the Magyars were defeated by Otto the Great and forced to stay put in the Hungarian plains, they turned their once-ferocious energy into more constructive channels. Mingling with the Slavic people who had earlier settled in Hungary, they went to work to develop the fertile land as well as its gold and silver mines. Conversions to Christianity began late in the 10th century. In 997 Stephen, whose father was the country's first ruler to be baptized, became head of government. Known for his piety and special care for the poor (he would later be canonized), Stephen worked with Pope Sylvester II (former tutor of Otto III) to set up an organized hierarchy so that the Church could firmly establish itself.

During his reign (997-1038) Stephen gave refuge to a member of the English royal family. A force of Danes had invaded England. The country's king, Edmund Ironside, was compelled in 1016 to share power with one of the invaders. Edmund died that same year, and his young son Edward escaped with his life and found welcome at the court of Hungary, far enough from England to avoid being victimized by the Danish usurper. Edward stayed in Hungary, where he grew up, married and had three children.

Back in England in the same year that Edward's daughter

Margaret was born, his uncle, now King Edward the Confessor, was forced to enter into a politically arranged marriage with the daughter of his greatest adversary. Edward was revered for his personal sanctity—witness the title of "Confessor"—but lacked the toughness to govern effectively in a turbulent age. As time passed with no heir (it's said the marriage was never consummated), the question of succession became a matter of concern to all parties connected with the throne.

DUNFERMLINE, SCOTLAND, OCTOBER 1068

Departing London by ship, 23-year-old Princess Margaret, her mother, younger brother and sister survive the voyage through a stormy North Sea. Once their coasting vessel heads inland along an estuary known as the Firth of Forth, the weather improves and the scenery too, for this is Scotland's golden autumn.

At his fortress-palace on a crag high above the firth, Malcolm Canmore, the king, gets word that the alien ship which has dropped anchor in the bay carries political refugees from England. He hurries to welcome them.

Margaret's family had deemed it wise to seek asylum in the nearest country. For the young Anglo-Saxon princess, being a political exile is hardly a novel experience. Until she was about 12, she had lived at the court of Hungary, since her father, though in the line of succession to the English throne, had not felt it safe to go back there. (Margaret's mother was a German princess related to the Hungarian royal family.) After Margaret's father received an invitation to return and was advised that he need no longer fear danger, he and the family journeyed to England. But he died almost immediately upon their arrival.

With close kin Edward the Confessor on the throne, the family elected to stay on. The English court was a friendly place to be—until the 1066 Norman Conquest brought a new, not-so-friendly king to power.

Had Margaret's brother Edgar been of hardier character, he might have attempted to recover the throne. As his father's heir, he did have a legitimate claim. Instead, the decision was made to look elsewhere for a home, bringing the family to Scotland and the court of Malcolm Canmore.

Malcolm himself had experienced exile as a boy. When his father was murdered in 1040 by Macbeth, he sought the protection of the English king for more than a dozen years, leaving when he was of an age to fight to reclaim the Scottish throne—just about the time that Margaret's family first arrived in England.

When Margaret and Malcolm meet, the king is in his late 30s, a widower with a son, and more than a little attracted to the young princess seeking his protection. As the *Anglo-Saxon Chronicle* puts it: "Then King Malcolm began to yearn for Edgar's sister as his wife."

Margaret's inclination has long been toward the contemplative life. Her sister Christina will later become abbess of an English monastery, which her mother will also join. Whatever the reason, however—perhaps to make life more secure for her family—Margaret finally gives in to the persistence of Malcolm who, though known for his tempestuous nature, never exhibits it with her. He can guess what marriage to her will be like, for her very first act as queen is to build a large church.

Next she addresses herself to the rather rustic ways of the court. The gently bred but strong-willed Margaret determines to soften the rough manners of the knights attached to service at the palace (though it is less palatial in appearance than fortress-like). Distressed that the men leave the table the moment they finish eating, she wants them at least to take time to say grace, a prayer of thanksgiving for the meal.

Rather than hurt their feelings with a lecture, she starts her crusade by arranging that the knights who follow her wishes will be offered a special cup of wine—the Grace Cup—sent to the table by her. Soon all the knights can be seen praying after mealtime. (For many years, the Grace Cup or St. Margaret's Blessing, as it was also called, was a feature of every Scottish festival.)

Nor does the queen neglect the ladies at court. She organizes them to study Scripture together and teaches them the *Opus Angelicum*, "Angel's Work," setting up in one of the great rooms of the castle a workshop for liturgical art. There the ladies make priestly vestments, altar linens and tapestries for church decoration.

Organizer that she is, Margaret has her own regime of work, study and prayer. Brought up under the influence of Benedictine ideas, she asks a Lincolnshire Benedictine monk named Turgot to be her chaplain. The biography he later writes supplies many of the personal details known about Margaret. Little is known, however, of the queen's physical appearance, except that she is tall. The beauty of her nature seems to count for more to the chroniclers. There must have been a radiance about her to which Malcolm duly responded, for it is said that "her loving spirit set his on fire."

Though unable to read or write, Malcolm, seeing the pleasure she derives from books, takes note of those she particularly likes, then has craftsmen embellish them with gold and precious gems. (Her most treasured book, her illuminated Gospel Book—though long since minus the richly ornamented cover—is preserved today in the Bodleian Library at Oxford University.)

Books represent Margaret's one personal extravagance. She is otherwise lavish only in the way she spends herself— and the royal treasury—in unflagging service to others, the poor foremost among them. Margaret takes seriously the words of her favorite books, the Gospels, and sees Christ in every person in need. She does more than go out to visit the poor and sick. Daily the court chamberlain is detailed to bring in six of the poorest people. Before feeding them, the queen washes their feet in the humble act of a slave. When Malcolm is at home, she persuades him to join her.

During the seasons of Lent and Advent, the royal hall is transformed into a great dining space for several hundred of the poor, who are provided the same kind of food and drink as the court enjoys. The queen helps serve down one side of the hall, the king on the other.

Throughout the year all her life Margaret regularly supports two dozen of the poor out of the state treasury. When that runs dry, she helps herself to her husband's personal funds. (Margaret's biographer wrote that "this pious plundering the king always took pleasantly and in good part.") She also convinces Malcolm to fund the almshouses and hospitals which she establishes.

Justice concerns her too. She insists that her husband do something to curb the soldiers' pillaging their own countrymen as well as to restrain the nobles from feuding among themselves. The violence must stop, she says, and he agrees, for Scotland has trouble enough just defending itself against that rich and powerful neighbor to the south.

Margaret is not above sending her own spies about the country to determine who among the Scots are mistreating captives taken in the skirmishes with England. If the situation warrants, she will pay the ransom required to set a captive free.

The Church of Scotland comes in for scrutiny too. It disturbs her that liturgical practices have crept in which differ from the rest of the Western Church, for she understands the tremendous unifying strength of a universal liturgy with the symbolic value of uniformity from one end of Europe to the other. As to people failing to receive the Eucharist, holding the sacrament in such awe that they feel too unworthy, she exclaims: "What! Shall no one that is a sinner taste that holy mystery? If so, then it follows that no one at all should receive it, for no one is pure from sin." Citing the gospel as well as commentaries by Church Fathers to convince the faithful of the graces available, she induces many to return to a reception of the Eucharist not only at Easter but on other feasts too.

Above all, the queen worries about the lukewarmness of the hierarchy and clergy toward their religion. She summons Church leaders to a synod—first to hear their point of view, then to explain her feelings, based on Scripture and other authoritative writings.

Prior to the synod, there had not been gatherings to

discuss country-wide Church policy. Now other councils
follow as Margaret attempts to correct abuses, promote
better education for the clergy and advance spirituality. An
account of one council session tells of Malcolm's presence to
provide backing for anything Margaret may choose to do.
But she is in charge and leads the discussion. According to
her biographer, the proud and able warrior is ready to bend
to his wife's will because he sees in her "the incarnation of all
that was pure and holy."

She is also the mother of their eight children. With all her
other responsibilities, Margaret finds time to instruct them
personally in their faith and to supervise their studies. To
accomplish so much, Margaret has learned to do with little
sleep.

At an indeterminate time the royal family moves its
residence across the Firth of Forth to Edinburgh on the south
shore, where Margaret spends many happy hours with her
children in the castle garden. In Edinburgh today, her
oratory on Castle Rock has the distinction of being the city's
oldest building. (The name *Edinburgh* comes from Edwin,
king of Northumbria. After conquering the district in the
seventh century, he built a fortress called Edwin's Burgh.
Edwin, you may remember, was the great-uncle of Hilda of
Whitby.)

The one cloud that darkens Margaret's life is the brutality
of warfare common to her time. On this she and Malcolm,
otherwise so close in spirit, do not agree. Where she sees
inhumanity, he sees necessity. When his country's
independence is at stake, no amount of eloquence on
Margaret's part bears weight.

Periodic invasions by England are countered with raids
into English territory by Malcolm's troops. (Some of the
raids, it deserves noting, are on behalf of Margaret's brother
Edgar, whose penchant for political intriguing gets him into
trouble. He regularly runs to Malcolm for help.)

As penance for the violence, Margaret fasts to extremes
despite her confessor Turgot's advice to the contrary. He
warns that her health will suffer.

A treaty between the two countries brings a temporary

peace, but in 1093 promises are broken and Malcolm must go off to war again. He takes his two oldest sons with him. As her health begins to fail rapidly and with a premonition that Malcolm's expedition will end in his death, Margaret summons Turgot, who had left the court two years before to become prior at Durham.

"There are two things which I beg of you," Margaret says to Turgot. She asks first to be remembered always in his prayers. "The other is that you will take some care about my sons and daughters. Lavish your affection upon them; teach them before all things to love and fear God; never cease instructing them." Turgot promises to abide by her wishes.

Margaret's worst fears are realized. Not only is Malcolm killed, but their eldest son too. After hearing the news, she dies within a matter of days. Margaret and Malcolm are both buried at Dunfermline Abbey, which the two had founded in the early years of their marriage.

AFTERWARD

Near Dunfermline is a stone called St. Margaret's Stone. Here, says tradition, the queen used to sit so that anyone in trouble might come to her. While this may not be literally true, it is likely founded on the fact that the public—including beggars—had easy access to her.

Acting always with exquisite courtesy toward each person, rich or poor, Margaret practiced the rare art of bringing about reform without ruffling feathers. In her reforms she led Scotland out of its previous isolation and into line with the rest of Western Christendom. A sense of a common community was developing throughout Europe. With Margaret began her country's integration into the cultural and religious society of Europe. Solidifying ties in the Church of the West meant all the more since, in 1054, the final break had come between Rome and the Orthodox Church of the East.

Margaret's sons, serving in turn as kings, carried on her policies, which inaugurated a golden age for Scotland that was to last 200 years.

Hildegard of Bingen

BACKGROUND

Christendom stretched from Scotland to the borders of Russia where in 957 Olga, duchess of Kiev, had become one of the first Russian converts. The sense of a kingdom crossing political boundaries was based on mutual sharing of Christian culture and values.

The 11th century had seen the papacy grow increasingly influential under a succession of strong popes capable of enforcing their decrees. In 1075, for instance, celibacy, which had long been an issue, became the norm when Pope Gregory VII insisted on it. Popes also took over calling Church councils. In the past, these had been held in the East, often at the behest of the emperor there. Since the final split between the Church of East and West in 1054, popes saw that councils met in the West and presided over them.

The spiritual vigor of Western Christendom could be viewed in the construction of cathedrals such as Notre Dame and a mounting veneration for the Virgin Mary (though women religious must now look to male authority for the last word). Other signs of new life were the founding of several reform-minded orders of monks. The Carthusians (1084) and Cistercians (1098) both aimed at combating laxities creeping in as the Cluniac movement lost its edge and became history. Some individuals called for a return to the simplicity of the Apostolic Age, accusing both papacy and clerics of spending too much time on temporal affairs, but their voices were muted—most often by ecclesiastical force.

The foregoing trends seemed to coalesce when Pope Urban II convened the Council of Clermont (France) in 1095 and issued his famous call for a Crusade to rescue the Holy Land from the infidel Turks. The response was immediate and enthusiastic. Such was the pope's authority as well as the fervor of the times. The great stain on that first Crusade came as the knights of Christendom, in their march eastward across the continent, stopped long enough to massacre European Jews by the tens of thousands.

TRIER, GERMANY, WINTER OF 1147-1148

Pope Eugenius III calls a synod during which the participants discuss the visions of a talked-about Rhineland nun, Hildegard of Bingen. A commission headed by the bishop of Verdun returns from its investigation of the nun to report: "I found her, Holy Father, as a flaming torch which our Lord has lighted in His Church." To which the pope replies, "Then we must not put it under a bushel."

He writes to Hildegard, letting her know that the synod has concluded her visions come from God, compliments her on being so favored but also cautions her against pride. In a letter of response Hildegard thanks the pope, then, referring to current abuses in the Church, tells Eugenius he must work harder to correct them.

Despite the sound of it, Hildegard never finds her role as reformer an easy one. As late as her 70s, when she is famous throughout Christendom for her gift of prophecy, she confides to a monk: "For my part I am always in fear and trembling because I have not any security as to what I am able to do." Only God's support sustains her, she explains, "as on wings whose flight is beyond comprehension and which soar in the heavens in spite of all contrary winds."

Had she followed her own inclinations, Hildegard might easily have remained in obscurity all of her life. Born in 1098 in a village 30 miles south of Bingen, Hildegard has been described as a "solitary and unusual child" who, at the age of eight, became her parents' "tithe to the Lord"—a not uncommon practice then (but more common when the youngster was "different"). Her father, a knight in the service of the local duke, placed his tenth child in the care of the duke's daughter Jutta. This holy and learned woman had chosen to live in a two-room cell adjoining the church of a Benedictine monastery in the neighborhood. The only other companion at St. Disibod was to be one of Jutta's poor cousins, there to aid with domestic chores.

Around the age of 15, Hildegard took vows as a nun. Quiet years of prayer, work and study followed. When Jutta died in 1136, Hildegard, at 38, was appointed superior, though much against her will, for the limelight was never what she sought. Jutta's original community had grown to about a dozen women living according to the Benedictine Rule. Although still located at Mount St. Disibod, they by then enjoyed a convent of their own.

Hildegard's health, never the best even in childhood, was afflicted still more by the interior struggles brought on by having to face exterior ordeals. Since at least the age of five, she experienced visions, seen not in a physical sense but with spiritual sight in the depths of her soul, gifting her with revelations and prophecies. The visions took their toll. So powerfully was her entire self claimed by communion with God, at times Hildegard thought she would break. To Bernard, the renowned abbot of Clairvaux, motherhouse of the reform-minded Cistercian Order, she once confessed that the visions burned her soul. (Of all the great figures of the 12th century, which Hildegard's life nearly spans, Bernard alone seems to have escaped a critical review by her. He was the most influential man of that era.)

Though often confined to bed for weeks at a time—and even when well, having difficulty walking—she continued her single-handed campaign to redirect the many worldly minds in the hierarchy and clergy to spiritual concerns. For any individual to embark on such a course takes rare courage. For a woman of her day, it was a double burden, and Hildegard knew it, complaining that she was "wretched and more than wretched in my existence as a woman."

The seemingly uneventful years that preceded her entrance onto the world stage were marked by mystical experience. Shy and sensitive by nature, she was scarcely ready to share her spiritual side with others, fearing that people were bound to laugh at her. Finally Hildegard told her confessor, who advised her to write down her visions and revelations.

The nun resisted until, as she explained, "I heard a voice from heaven which said to me, 'Relate these marvels; write down the things which thou has learnt and say, in the year 1141 of the Incarnation of the Son of God, at the age of 42 years, 7 months, a fiery light of wondrous brightness coming from the open heavens, dispersed itself all about my Brain and all about my heart and all about my Breast as a flame; yet not such as burns, but such as warms....' " And then she describes being illuminated with understanding.

This prompted her to begin writing her first and most celebrated book, *Scito vias Domini* ("Know the Ways of the Lord"), often referred to by its abbreviated title, *Scivias*. The work took almost 10 years to complete. Meanwhile, the woman destined to tackle major problems in Church and society found herself doing battle first with the abbot of Mount St. Disibod.

Her community has grown to more than 50 women and present convent quarters prove too cramped. Because the Disibod monks' need for more space has already made a big dent in what is available, Hildegard decides on a move to Mount St. Rupert, a site much closer to Bingen.

Technically the nuns owe obedience to the abbot, and he strongly opposes the idea. The thought of losing Hildegard along with her newfound prestige (and the income that might result) upsets his plans. As habitually happens, Hildegard's health soon suffers—until, in a vision, God commands the move. The pope subsequently gives his approval for a new convent.

Reassured, Hildegard recovers sufficiently to oversee the construction at Rupertsberg, including one innovative feature: plumbing that pipes water for use inside the building. (Like all authentic mystics, she knows when it is time to come back down to earth.)

As a way of forestalling future problems with the abbot, she initiates the lengthy process of putting Rupertsberg under the protection of the archbishop at Mainz, and eventually the request is granted.

The move to the new convent takes place in 1150, and the community begins to flourish as never before. These nuns are a talented lot—women of considerable creativity in music and the arts. Under Hildegard's direction they illuminate manuscripts including, possibly, the magnificent ones in *Scivias* which depict the abbess's visions. (Another possibility is that the illustrations were produced by friends who were monks at an abbey in Trier, but still done under her supervision.)

Hildegard also composes dozens of hymns and writes the first known morality play, *Ordo Virtutum* ("The Ritual of the Virtues"). The play deals with the mystery of good and evil in life. Set to music, it has sometimes been compared to opera. (The play is still being performed.)

Other writings include commentaries on the Gospels, biographies of St. Rupert and St. Disibod, Celtic missionaries to the Rhineland in earlier centuries, several more books dealing with her visions, as well as books on natural history and medicines—one of these of encyclopedic proportions.

Hildegard's interest in the study of medicine stems from her own chronic experience with illness, and some of her theories come surprisingly close to later scientific discoveries, such as one on the circulation of blood. Her monastery garden blooms with medicinal herbs, which are not reserved for nuns only but available also to sick people from the surrounding area who show up at the infirmary in anticipation of the abbess's healing ways. She is said to have mastered the art of doctoring.

Many other visitors seeking advice on spiritual matters,

princes of the Church and humble pilgrims, too, appear on the doorstep. Then there are those the monastery makes room for as permanent residents—poor, older women—so that "the evening of their life should be good," according to one biographer who lived for years in the neighborhood.

What with her books and a voluminous correspondence, Hildegard now requires the help of two secretaries to whom she dictates. One is her longtime friend, Volmar, a monk at Mount St. Disibod, who acts in this capacity until his death in 1773; the other is Richarda, a favorite among her nuns.

Once the Rupertsberg community is well established, she feels free to go out on apostolic journeys, to deliver her prophetic words in person. In her 50s Hildegard takes to the road, traveling about Germany by horseback (in her 70s she goes to France). Because the roads are not safe, an armed escort accompanies her.

Though on the surface the 12th century appears to be a great one for Western Christendom, with the authority of the papacy firmly grounded, Hildegard looks deeper, sees all that's wrong and becomes convinced of the absolute necessity to speak out no matter what the personal cost. Not having sought the gift of prophecy, she admits to finding it a "painful job."

Wearing a black habit (she wears white only for the great feasts), the abbess makes a powerful impression as she ascends pulpits in both cathedrals and religious communities to attack the evils of corruption and a too luxurious life-style among the clergy. She commends only those who prove themselves soldiers for Christ.

Hildegard pictures the ailing Church as a weeping mother in pain. In forceful language she accuses bishops and abbots of preferring a sword to a shepherd's staff, letting their involvement in secular business—the administration of monastic lands, for example—take precedence over spiritual guidance of their flock. The laity, she admonishes Church leaders, suffer as a result. Opposition there may be when her words prick consciences, but Hildegard also instills in some the courage to make changes, infusing her own ardor for greater commitment, and brings reassurance to the faithful.

Many hear "the voice of Christ" in her prophesying.

When clergy in Cologne request a copy of a speech, she sends with it a letter in which she tells of being "completely exhausted" from her round of speech-making. The nun indicates too an ability to smile at herself, noting with wry amusement that though nothing but a shy, poor woman, she is in the absurd situation of lecturing "wise men" who hold degrees as Masters of Arts and Doctors.

Hildegard offers an insightful look in comparing herself to Judith, the apocryphal woman of the Old Testament, who single-handedly slew the Assyrian general threatening to destroy Israel and thereby brought peace to her people. As the story of that victory goes: "...but the Lord Almighty has thwarted them by a woman's hand."

Whether by letter or direct encounter, Hildegard confronts the greatest leaders of her era: Henry II of England, remembered as the king responsible for the murder of Archbishop Thomas à Becket; Henry's wife, Eleanor of Acquitane; and German emperors, including Conrad III and the fearsome Frederick Barbarossa, who invites her to his palace.

The century was plagued by nearly a dozen antipopes as kings and emperors made futile attempts to regain control of the papacy. On one occasion, when Barbarossa decides to name an antipope, Hildegard fires off a letter denouncing his action as that of a "madman."

A fighter to the literal end, her last great battle with the power structure calls attention to an often overlooked spirit of compassion as well as her sense of justice. She runs into trouble with canons at Mainz Cathedral because of a situation that comes about when a young man is allowed burial in the Rupertsberg cemetery. Though he had been excommunicated by the archbishop (whom Hildegard had already reproved for living the good life in Italy instead of residing in the archdiocese), the abbess, whose love excluded no one, is of the firm belief that the man truly repented. Since he had received the last sacraments before his death, he must certainly have made his peace with God. What is more, a vision confirms her belief.

Nevertheless, ecclesiastical officials order her to remove the body from sacred ground. When she refuses, her convent is threatened with interdict: No Masses will be said, no sacraments given to her community, no liturgical music sung—and she loves her music. Even the church bells cannot be rung.

Eighty-year-old Hildegard goes out to the cemetery and with her walking staff erases the lines around the young man's grave so that his burial place cannot be detected. A furious archbishop gets the pope to agree to the interdict.

The impasse drags on for a year, causing Hildegard immense sorrow, but she remains resolute. Only after protracted negotiations and the intercession of influential friends is the ban withdrawn. Hildegard dies just a few months later, in September 1179.

AFTERWARD

Certainly one of the major figures of her time, Hildegard left her mark on the 12th century with an extraordinary range of achievements. Had she been only a mystic and writer of spiritual literature, or only a theologian and scientist, or only an artist and musician, or only a prophet and reformer, her life would have been remarkable enough. But she was all of the above!

The flavor of her prophesying, incidentally, may be found in passages on the fate of the wicked which have been compared to descriptions in Dante's *Inferno*, written about a hundred years later.

In overcoming the "handicap," as Hildegard saw it, of being a woman in basically a man's world, she served as the conscience of the Church. In her mysticism she led the way as the first of the great Rhineland mystics. She left a legacy of music as well as inspired writings. In some ways—her concern for the environment as exemplified by a creation-centered theology—Hildegard is almost more 20th-century than 12th. For what is more contemporary than her observation: "All nature is at the disposal of humankind. We are to work with it. Without it we cannot survive"?

Her reputation as a prophet of apocalyptic dimensions may tend to overshadow the essential nature of this otherwise shy woman. She summed up her personal philosophy in quite gentle terms: What the individual heart needs is to be flooded with love, and what the Church needs is to be holy.

Clare of Assisi

BACKGROUND

"**U**ndiminished vitality" aptly
describes the 13th century, which is also often called "the
greatest of centuries" for Western Christendom. Never again
would the papacy achieve quite such supremacy in both the
sacred and secular realm. One of the greatest popes,
Innocent III, was elected while still in his 30s and proved
admirably effective as churchman and statesman as well.
There was much to oversee since a considerable bureaucracy
had by now been created to administer the manifold
responsibilities of the Church.

This took money. Peter's Pence, conceived earlier, was
only a start. Next, taxes were levied on churches around
Christendom to help pay the bills.

There was money to be had, especially in Italy, for its
towns prospered as a result of the East-West trade and travel
(including pilgrimage) engendered by the Crusades. Venice,
for example, served as the chief embarkation port for the
Holy Land. But even in the comparatively small town of
Assisi in the Umbrian Hills of central Italy, an ever-
expanding merchant class was ready to challenge the power
of local feudal lords. Though peasants still constituted the
majority of the population in Europe, society was in
transition.

Amid all the exuberance of the era, many of the laity

viewed with dissatisfaction the sight of a Church grown mighty in its wealth and consequent worldliness. It seemed to contradict the very gospel values it preached. A longing to see a return to the purity of authentic gospel living began to stir.

ASSISI, ITALY, MARCH 18, 1212

Eighteen-year-old Clare di Favarone slips away Palm Sunday night from her parents' home to meet the 30-year-old preacher, Francis Bernardone, in the woods outside the town walls. She is accompanied by a trusted friend; he, by his band of Poor Brothers carrying burning torches. They enter the Chapel of St. Mary of the Angels and, before the altar, Clare renounces the world, consecrating herself to God. Francis cuts off her long golden hair; she lays aside the jewels she wears and exchanges her elegant gown for a garment of gray sackcloth.

Once this has been accomplished, however, a question arises: What will Francis do with her now? Her family's reaction is bound to be stormy. Her father, of the landed aristocracy, had planned marriage for his beautiful and intelligent daughter, though ever since Clare first heard Francis preach of Jesus' love and the joy of holy poverty, she has yearned to join his company. To that end, she had been meeting him secretly for the past year—always with a companion to chaperone her properly.

Until more definite arrangements can be made, Francis places Clare in a nearby convent. Her family soon discovers that she has run off, apparently under the influence of that (some say crazy) son of the cloth merchant, whose recently organized company of friars beg for their daily bread. A contingent of male relatives shows up at the convent to bring the young woman home. They are scandalized to see her with shorn hair, barefoot and dressed like the poorest peasant. Clare absolutely refuses to let them take her back.

The nuns Francis talked into harboring Clare decide they do not need that kind of trouble, and he finds a second convent for her. Here one of Clare's younger sisters, 15-year-old Agnes, joins her. The family, understandably upset that two of their daughters are now in the hands of the wandering preacher, create an even bigger disturbance. Again they fail. These nuns too want no more of such goings-on. Clare herself is happy about leaving, for she has been at this convent just long enough to observe the nuns wrangling with the bishop over the community's commercial farming enterprise. She has different ideas about religious life for women.

Francis, having obtained permission from Benedictines who own the property, next takes the two young women to a little house beside the Church of San Damiano. This was the church he had rebuilt after hearing the voice of the Lord say, "Francis, go and rebuild my church, for it is in need of repair." Taking the instruction literally—just as he does with gospel teachings—he had done his best to mend the tumbledown building. San Damiano remains close to Francis' heart, therefore making it special to Clare.

The accommodations at San Damiano are a far cry from what Favarone's daughters are accustomed to. Despite the austere surroundings, they are soon joined by other young friends and kinswomen from the noble families of Assisi who find Francis' message irresistible, for he practices what he preaches (penance, poverty and joy).

Perhaps Clare dreamed fleetingly of walking in his footsteps in the same manner as the dozen or so members of the brotherhood. But even the idealistic Francis recognizes the impossibility of a woman—let alone a high-born one—tramping about Italy, begging for her daily bread. No, convent life in some form is the only practical solution.

But, as Clare will insist to her dying breath, it must be a life of absolute poverty—even though the Church itself has difficulty with the idea. By now, ecclesiastical holdings constitute more than half the lands of Europe. In religious orders members may vow poverty in the sense of retaining no possessions as individuals, yet they hold collective ownership of income-producing property such as agricultural land. This property, often given as an endowment to a convent or monastery, ensures its financial stability. But Clare and her Poor Ladies aim to hold only enough land to maintain the privacy of their monastery and to cultivate only enough garden to supply the needs of the sisters' table.

All her life, Clare will be ready to stand up to those who in theory have power over her, but when Francis says she is to live an enclosed existence of some sort, she accepts it, as long as that life adheres faithfully to the gospel. The two are twin souls, finding their security in Providence rather than possessions.

The time is right for a venture such as theirs, for the 13th century is a spirited age. The people of Western Christendom build soaring cathedrals, engage in feudal wars, go on Crusades or aspire to join the growing class of merchants and artisans. The majority of the population still belongs to the peasantry, and there exists a great gap between them and Church officials, who often seem to prefer high living to high ideals. The general mood among the more pious-minded laity becomes one of disenchantment with the institutional Church. Out of this has sprung popular religious movements of varying types. Francis' own little company begins as a lay movement, though he humbly agrees to ordination as a deacon in order to preach the gospel.

This then is the state of affairs when Pope Innocent III takes time from a heavy schedule to hear the petition of a group which has come to Rome seeking approval of a new order to be known as the Friars Minor. Their leader appears insignificant enough, but the pope senses something about the man. In another few years, around 1215, Innocent will find himself also approving the Rule of an associated group, the Poor Ladies. Clare asks the pope to grant them the privilege of possessing nothing; in agreeing, he observes with wonder that such a privilege has never been asked of Rome before.

In its first years, before papal sanction, San Damiano

operates rather informally, coming under Francis' personal direction. He provides the women with a very simple rule of life which emphasizes, as Clare records in her Testament, "that we should persevere always in holy poverty."

The nuns support the friars' active apostolate with contemplative prayer. The brethren in turn beg alms for the Poor Ladies. When at one point a pope forbids visitation by friars assigned as chaplains unless given permission for the particular occasion, Clare decrees that neither will the men who regularly beg for them be allowed in the cloister to deliver the daily bread and other contributions. She argues that the spiritual food provided by chaplains is just as necessary to the women as the material kind. The order is quickly rescinded.

Though prayer serves as the focus of the nuns' vocation, Clare believes in manual work too. The women do household chores, cultivate a small vegetable garden, spin cloth to make altar linens and nurse the sick brought to them, including any lepers Francis might send to have their sores bathed and bandaged.

Clare's charitable impulses developed early. As a child she found ways to give her own meals to the poor on many occasions. And when converted by Francis, she resourcefully managed to distribute her entire inheritance to the needy. (She may have had an ally in her devout mother, Ortolano. Sometime after the death of Favarone, she, too, joined the Poor Ladies. So did Clare's youngest sister, Beatrice.)

When the order is formalized in 1215, a reluctant Clare, for she is scarcely 21, accedes to Francis' naming her abbess. (She calls herself "the little plant of the most blessed Father Francis.") Unlike the traditional religious superior of the time, Clare sees her role of abbess as one of servant to her sisters. Among the ways she does this is by washing the feet of the lay sisters, those nuns who are permitted outside the cloister to attend to convent errands. No ritual footwashing this, for the sisters come back from walking barefoot along muddy country lanes and garbage-strewn city streets. One of Francis' first friars, Thomas of Celano, reports in his biography of Clare that "she never shrank from any menial task, so that at the table she usually poured water on the hands of the Sisters, assisted those who were sitting, and served those who were eating. She herself washed and cleansed the commodes of the sick Sisters, making nothing of it, minding not the filth or the odor."

Where the welfare of her Poor Ladies is concerned, Clare shows maternal solicitude: going through the dormitory at night to pull blankets over sleeping sisters, allowing feather pillows for the ailing and ordering woolen stockings for those especially sensitive to the cold. In the early years Clare herself practices austerities she warns the others against: rigorous fasting (three days a week she eats nothing), wearing a hair shirt (a practice dating to her pre-convent days), sleeping on vine twigs with a stone for a pillow.

When worried nuns tell Francis what she's been doing, he insists that she moderate her ways, making sure first of all that she has a mattress and pillow stuffed with straw. Clare's mortifications can only be understood in terms of her ardent love for God and the matching desire to express it in heroic fashion. Both Clare and Francis will realize too late, when their health begins to fail, that they have overdone a good thing.

Clare's love takes in all of God's creation, including her pet cat. She has a hole cut in the refectory door of the convent so that the cat can come in for meals. (The animal's special entrance is still pointed out to visitors at San Damiano.)

In 1219 the two persons dearest to Clare's heart each take leave of Assisi. Her sister Agnes is sent to a religious community near Florence to instill the spirit of the Poor Ladies. This is the first of more than a hundred similar monasteries to be established during Clare's lifetime. The two sisters will not see each other again until the abbess is on her deathbed years later.

Francis departs too, on an impetuous journey to the Holy Land in hopes of converting the Saracens to Christianity. He leaves other friars in charge at home. The brotherhood has now grown to 5,000 members, many of whom feel that Francis' ideal is simply no longer practical. While he is away, they set about "regularizing" the friars into a more traditional structure, acquiring property and eliminating absolute poverty. They attempt to do the same with the Poor Ladies, but Clare will have none of it.

When Francis returns, with his health already deteriorating, and discovers that a new rule for Franciscans is about to be approved, he in effect withdraws from administration of the order. In 1225 he retires for nearly two months to San Damiano, where Clare has a hut built in the garden for the ailing Francis. Amid her favorite flowers— lilies, roses and violets—he composes "The Canticle of Brother Sun" and also a hymn in praise of the Poor Ladies. After this peaceful interlude, he receives the stigmata, and Clare makes him a special pair of slippers to relieve the pain of the wounds.

Before his death in 1226, he asks that she remain faithful to the poverty they both believe in. She will keep the promise despite the best attempts of several powerful popes who, though they admire the abbess tremendously, wish her to modify the Rule at least a little. After all, the friars have done so.

Two years after Francis' death, Pope Gregory IX, who had been a friend in his cardinal days, insists on endowing the Second Order with land and a building. In a celebrated interview he suggests releasing her from the "absolute" part of her vow of poverty to ease her conscience about accepting property. Clare refuses to accept anything and tells the pope: "Holy Father, never do I wish to be released in any way from the following of Christ." Gregory finds himself yielding, and in a subsequent letter to her (September 17, 1228) makes it official: "We confirm your resolution to live in the utmost poverty."

Even without the beloved Francis as ally, life must go on. Clare continues as abbess notwithstanding her growing infirmities. On occasion the nuns have to lift her up so that she can spin wool and linen. During several harrowing incidents, however, it is Clare who gives her sisters support— of a moral kind.

The first occasion is when Assisi gets caught in the crossfire between the Papal States of central Italy and

Frederick II of Germany. In the political maze of the times, the emperor also has dominion over Sicily, where his subjects include Saracens, who had once controlled that island. Frederick recruits them into his army. While on mission for him in the Umbrian hills, they go on a pillaging raid. As they scale the outer walls of San Damiano late at night, their blood-curdling cries terrify the sisters, who rush to Clare's sickbed. Helped up, she prays, then turns to the women and says, "My daughters and sisters, do not be afraid, for the Lord will defend you. I will be hostage for you." Ready to die for them, she takes the silver box containing the Blessed Sacrament to an open window. By now the Saracens have placed a ladder against the building itself but, at sight of the majestic Clare, they suddenly, miraculously, take flight.

The following year, imperial soldiers are again in the area, planning to plunder Assisi. As the citizens organize to defend themselves, Clare and her nuns pray for deliverance of the city. These soldiers also unaccountably flee in disorder. The people of Assisi are forever grateful to the Poor Ladies for the strength of their prayers.

A feeling for the kind of prayer life that went on at San Damiano can be gained from Thomas of Celano's contemporary description of the abbess who led them: "When Clare returned with joy from holy prayer, she brought with her burning words from the fire of the altar of the Lord, which enkindled the hearts of the sisters. They marveled indeed that such sweetness came from her lips while her face shone more radiantly than usual."

Clare's years of praying that the Franciscan ideal may be preserved by her Second Order find fulfillment two days before her death, when the Rule she has written to confirm absolute poverty receives official papal approval. When the document is delivered to her, eyewitnesses say that she "took it reverently into her hands and kissed it many times."

AFTERWARD

For more than 40 years, until her death in 1253, Clare was shut away from the world. She was cloistered but not sheltered, for popes came to visit her at San Damiano and queens wrote to her for advice. Agnes of Bohemia was the first member of royalty to enter a Poor Ladies community, after turning down offers of marriage from such suitors as Frederick II. Some of Clare's letters to Agnes on the spiritual life reveal in her own words how love permeated her prayer. Physically enclosed, Clare's spirit soared.

Together with Francis, Clare refreshed the entire Church, and the effects are still being felt. The achievements of one can never be mentioned without the other. Theirs is one of the outstanding examples in Christianity of a pure and perfect friendship. One suspects that Clare was most in Francis' mind when he once told some friars his feelings toward the Poor Ladies: "Do not believe, dearest brothers, that I do not love them perfectly."

The Franciscan ideal—preserving the heart of the gospel through loving service—was Clare's gift to Francis and the Church. She never failed her cherished friend. The Friars Minor and Poor Clares (as her order came to be called) gave rise to a Third Order: people of their day who wanted to live in the Franciscan way even though circumstances prohibited their entering a religious community. First called Brothers and Sisters of Penance, these groups of lay men and women spread rapidly across Europe. (Queen Elizabeth of Hungary was among the first members.) The importance of this to the spiritual life of the laity in the Middle Ages was immense.

Catherine of Siena

BACKGROUND

The 14th century began on a note of celebration when Pope Boniface VIII declared the year 1300 a "Jubilee Year" for Rome. (The nightmare of the Black Death still lay ahead; it first appeared in 1347.) Pilgrims from around Christendom were invited to visit the Roman shrines and churches dedicated to Saints Peter and Paul—and leave their offerings. For Boniface saw the occasion as a great way to raise funds. Failing to reckon with rising nationalistic feelings in Europe, he also envisioned putting papal power on display.

In his dealings with secular rulers Boniface knew how to antagonize—especially Philip IV, king of France. That was a mistake, for in a contest of power, Philip would come out ahead of the 86-year-old Boniface.

Soon after Boniface's death, Philip managed to get a French pope elected—one who preferred living closer to home. The papal court was therefore removed to Avignon which, though not then officially part of France but situated just across its border, fell under the domination of the king. Thus began what history terms the "Babylonian Captivity," during which the papacy lost not only its international standing in temporal affairs but its moral authority, too. Transferring the court moreover proved an expensive proposition. It required building anew a city worthy of the court, adding taxes on religious orders as well as the laity. This did nothing to increase a pope's popularity.

Great spiritual lights such as Dante Alighieri (who was also deeply involved in the politics of Florence) and Bridget of Sweden tried to persuade the papacy to return to Rome, but failed. They were a sign, though, that at a very low point for the institutional Church, Christianity could yet soar in spirituality. In one of those marvelous paradoxes of Church history, the 14th century witnessed an unparalleled flowering of the mystic life among individual Christians.

AVIGNON, JUNE 18, 1376

Preceded by her reputation, the young woman and her party from Siena go ashore. A small boat has taken them up the Rhone River on the last stage of their journey from Italy. Standing on the quay, they can see the towers and spires of the palace and the other magnificent buildings belonging to the papal court, which has been in residence here ever since 1308—much too long, in Catherine's opinion.

When received by the pope two days later, she gives no sign of being overawed by her surroundings or by the man she faces. Catherine has written Gregory XI often enough in the past, addressing him at times as *dolce babbo*, "sweetest father," imploring him always to move back to Italy, to the Papal States, where the head of the Church belongs. Meeting her now in person, Gregory waits to hear what this frail, impassioned woman has to say.

Catherine comes directly to the point: "To the glory of Almighty God I am bound to say that I smelled the stink of the sins which flourish in the papal court while I was still at home in my own town more sharply than those who have practiced them, and do practice them, every day here." (She has had several days to observe.)

Her spiritual adviser serves as interpreter, since the pope

is French and Catherine speaks only her native Tuscan. Lack of formal education and lack of an aristocratic background (Catherine's father was a cloth-dyer) are not enough to hold her back, however.

Gregory recognizes the truth of her words as well as the obvious holiness that animates her. Despite her urgent call to action, he vacillates. For pious though the pope may be, courage characteristically fails him. There are just too many pressures coming from the powerful French king, the luxury-loving French cardinals and the vast number of hangers-on who have no desire to leave the opulence of Avignon for the ruins called Rome. Undeterred by such formidable forces, Catherine continues to argue the issue. Her beloved Church is in peril and she feels called by God to do what she can to save it.

In the nearly 70 years since a French king managed to shift the papal court to Avignon, the papacy has been reduced to a political tool. In a century marked by the Hundred Years' War between England and France, recurrent epidemics of the Black Death throughout Europe and interminable feuding among Italy's various city-states, Christian society needs spiritual guidance more than ever. Yet even the monasteries, Catherine tells Gregory, are "stables of swine." The only way the pope can purify the Church is by leaving the corrupting influence of Avignon and thus escape domination by kings. Back in his own Papal States, Gregory will be free to act independently and achieve reform.

He must think about it.

Meanwhile, when Catherine is not engaged in efforts to persuade, she prays. And when her devotions are public—as at Mass—she attracts the considerable curiosity of the women at court, who include both relatives of the prelates and their mistresses. Some take Catherine seriously; others seem afraid of this reformer and still others make fun of her.

Revered as a mystic by the band of disciples who have accompanied her to Avignon, she is gifted with visions and subject to trances. Seeing her in the chapel one day, prostrate on the floor after falling into a trance, one young woman who is married to the pope's nephew sticks a large needle into Catherine's foot to determine whether it is really true that the mystic feels nothing while divinely transported. After regaining consciousness, Catherine begins to experience so much pain that she is unable to stand on the wounded foot for several days.

At the end of three months, Gregory succumbs to her logic, and starts the journey to Rome. At the port of Marseilles, Catherine makes sure he boards the ship for Genoa. At Genoa, he arranges to meet her again secretly for added encouragement to go on. At long last she is free to return to Siena, where she regularly nurses the sick, assists the poor and visits those in prison. This Catherine does in spite of persistent ill health—always doing what she believes necessary, a trait that has marked her since childhood.

Youngest of the 25 children born to Jacopo and Monna Lapa Benincasa, Catherine made a vow of virginity at the age of seven. Even then, the happy-natured little girl showed evidence of a strong spiritual bent. Her parents allowed her to fast and do penances as she chose, for they were devout themselves. But when she reached the marriageable age of 13, the heretofore obedient Catherine absolutely refused to marry the young man Jacopo had in mind for her. In hopes of bringing about a change, he and Monna Lapa began imposing menial household chores on their adored daughter, leaving her little time for prayer. The single-minded girl found she could retreat into her interior "cell" as she worked. And rather than hold a grudge against the family (for brothers and sisters took to taunting her), she waited on them as though they were the Holy Family. Seeing the very best in everyone was to become a lifelong habit for her.

Finally the parents relented and, at 16, Catherine was accepted as a member of the local Dominican Third Order, even though its membership was then ordinarily restricted to widows. These tertiaries took no vows but lived in their own homes, dedicating themselves to charitable works. As their badge of identification, the women wore a white habit and black mantle.

With the approval of her spiritual director, Catherine spent the next three years in the solitude of her little room: praying and fasting, doing sacred reading, sleeping on a bare board and going out only to attend Mass. Never one to neglect friends, though, she wove wreaths of flowers which she sent them as greetings.

Hearing a call from God to begin her apostolic labors, Catherine reentered the world. Her kind of holiness, her joy in serving others, soon attracted a following. Two of her original disciples were sister members of the Third Order, but male disciples from all ranks of life joined her band too. Jacopo Benincasa granted use of the family home as the base of operations.

The neighbors talked, of course, when they saw numbers of men going in and out of the Benincasa house at all hours of the day and night, and young Catherine freely going about the town with them. She had no time to worry about talk (which did eventually subside); she was too busy not only with missions of charity but also meeting a growing demand for her services as a peacemaker, healing rifts within families and between feuding families, a particular problem of the time.

Shortly after her father's death, a revolution broke out in the region. It lasted just long enough to affect the family fortunes as well as the local economy. Catherine's brothers had to look elsewhere for work and somehow, out of all that large family, she was the one to assume responsibility for the care of their mother. Thereafter, when Catherine traveled on peacemaking errands, Monna Lapa was found among the company of disciples.

There was little time for travel in 1374, though, for the Black Death—bubonic plague—made its second appearance in Siena. During an earlier epidemic, soon after Catherine's birth, Siena had lost one-third of its population. The disease continued to ravage Europe in waves, decimating the ranks of clergymen (which accounts for some of the Church's problems). The lower clergy willingly worked among the afflicted despite the danger. When Catherine joined in the effort, she met a priest, Raymond of Capua, who became her spiritual director and cherished friend for the rest of her short life. As the plague intensified, death carts made the rounds of the city each day to pick up the latest victims. Among them were two brothers and a sister of Catherine, and eight of the 11 grandchildren her mother had been raising.

When the epidemic ended, Catherine resumed her role of diplomat, answering first a call from the citizens of Pisa. Having shown an ability to reconcile feuding parties, she now got requests for help in settling differences between the various city-states of the Italian peninsula. Vying with each other for economic and political power, these independent republics—and the papacy too—hired mercenary soldiers to wage their wars. Prelates and others in authority found it almost impossible to believe that a young woman could be capable of conducting negotiations—until they met Catherine. While in Pisa, she heard that some of the cities were forming a league. To her sorrow, this new-found unity came about in order to fight the Holy See.

At the heart of the trouble was the city of Florence, at odds with the pope, who angrily placed Florence under interdict, ordering that its trade be cut off—the lifeblood of Florentine wealth. And here Catherine got involved. In 1376 the Florentines ask her to intercede for them, and she heads for Avignon—bringing us back to the start of our story.

While the officials of Florence mean only to use her as a pawn in a political game and, in effect, to leave her in the lurch when their own aims are met, an undismayed Catherine takes advantage of the circumstances to achieve her own long-held dream of getting the pope back to Rome.

The thoroughly French Pope Gregory discovers Rome is not to his liking and, as a consequence, develops a certain coolness toward Catherine. While working among the needy again in Siena—and in her spare time, founding a monastery for women—she gets a call from the pope in the early spring of 1378, asking her to go to Florence once more. Scarcely has she arrived there when news comes of Gregory's death. But a new pope, Urban, is named within 10 days, and he wants her to carry on.

With pro-papal and anti-papal factions doing violence to each other in Florence, Catherine gets blamed for the excesses of those who champion the pope. She and some friends are confronted in a garden one day by a mob demanding with drawn swords "that cursed Catherine." She steps forward to tell them, "Do what you will to me, but don't harm the people with me." The leader of the group then advises her to flee. She replies: "No, I will not," adding that she is ready to die if it will promote peace. The mob instead retreats. Catherine remains in the vicinity of Florence until an acceptable peace settlement has been concluded.

Back in Siena with her faithful disciples, the inveterate letter-writer to popes and princes turns her attention to a different form of writing. In the space of three months she dictates her *Divine Dialogue*, a spiritual guide described as "the love song of the soul and God, of Catherine and her Beloved." So fast does her mind work that she keeps three secretaries busy taking dictation.

While working on the book, she learns that the French have elected a rival pope. Pope Urban, though morally above reproach, has been proving utterly tactless in his dealings with people. Catherine writes him: "For the love of Jesus crucified, Holy Father, soften a little the sudden movements of your temper."

Urban summons Catherine to Rome to help rally support in his favor. Spending the last months of her life in Rome, she sends letter after letter to European rulers and prelates of the opposition party. Trying to save the papacy from disaster, she also addresses the Sacred College of Cardinals, urging them to have faith. When she concludes, Urban says to them: "This poor little woman puts us to shame by her courage."

Catherine foresees schism facing the Church. Her always fragile health fails rapidly. She suffers two strokes and—some say—a broken heart. Near the end, she tells her disciples: "Love one another, my children, love one another! For by this shall you show that you have had me and own me for mother."

AFTERWARD

When Catherine died at 33,
she genuinely believed herself a failure. Yet she had single-
handedly changed the course of history by ending the
Babylonian Captivity. Had this great peacemaker lived,
perhaps the Great Schism that rent the Church might have
been headed off. Instead, it would eventually produce three
popes, each one asking for obedience as well as
contributions. Only a general council called at Constance
finally ended the long schism in 1417.

In her brief day, Catherine was the most powerful
woman in Europe. Like Hildegard of Bingen before her, she
served as conscience of the Church when it was in dire need
of one. The people of Siena realized her worth, venerating
Monna Lapa (who lived to the age of 90) as the mother of a
saint. Two of her male disciples went on to become heads of
their orders: Dominican Raymond of Capua and Carthusian
Stefano Maconi.

Institutional problems of the Church aside, the 14th
century of Christianity was distinguished for its surge of
mystical development, and Catherine was one of the most
outstanding in a line of outstanding mystics. The theology
presented in her brilliant *Dialogue*, considered a jewel in
Italian religious literature, eventually earned for this
"unlettered" woman the title "Doctor of the Church"—a title
given to only one other woman in history. Above all,
Catherine showed what heights could be attained by one
individual grounded in prayer and motivated by love of God
and humanity.

Catherine of Genoa

BACKGROUND

Through both trade and the Crusades, Europeans had made close contact with the Islamic civilization of the East, one far advanced in science and the arts. Moreover, Muslim scholars had been busy rediscovering and preserving the classics of Greek and Roman antiquity. New ideas (regular bathing was one) as well as ancient learning found their way back to Europe, triggering the Renaissance.

It started in Florence, the city-state emerging as the hub of international banking. While other parts of Europe were developing into nations, Italian cities remained independent republics. The wealthiest families in each city-state assumed control, often passing down power to succeeding generations.

Prosperous Florentine bankers were among the first to invest in the arts. Such was the spirit of the times in Florence that the most talked-about event there in 1401 was a design competition for a set of sculptured doors for the town baptistery.

In the preoccupation with creating art and making money, scarcely a European brow was lifted when Constantinople appealed to the West for help as the Ottoman Turks besieged the city. The last official Crusade to defeat the infidels was long past, and so was interest in mounting another one, even though Pope Pius II offered to lead it himself. He tried in vain to rally Western rulers to the cause. Virtually the only response came from the merchants of Genoa, anxious that something be done lest they lose their trading rights in Constantinople in a Turkish takeover. Clearly that was not response enough. Constantinople, the last bastion of Eastern Christendom, fell in 1453.

REPUBLIC OF GENOA, JANUARY 13, 1463

With "the utmost repugnance," Catherine Fiesca signs the marriage contract. From all appearances, the groom shares her sentiments. Not made in heaven, this marriage is rather arranged by Catherine's older brother, head of the family since their father's death a few years earlier. The wedding ceremony itself will be celebrated at a later date in the Cathedral of San Lorenzo, across the way from the Fieschi Palazzo, where the couple will reside for the first two years.

What the marriage actually celebrates is a binding-up of political wounds. The two families that Catherine and Giuliano represent have been on opposite, warring sides, and the resultant civil disturbances threatened to undermine Genoese prosperity if the situation is not resolved.

No matter how 16-year-old Catherine looks upon the arrangement, tradition dictates that her brother's authority may not be questioned. So little heed is paid to her feelings, in fact, that no one bothers to tell her until the date and place of the ceremony have already been set.

She and young Giuliano come from similar backgrounds of wealth and social position, but they are otherwise totally unsuited. She, quiet and of a penitential nature, had attempted at 13 to enter a convent but was refused because of her age. He, hot-tempered and self-indulgent, finds her tastes disagreeable, though for the most part he seems scarcely to give his wife a second thought. During the next 10 years, he is often absent and unfaithful as well, as he later confesses.

Catherine's first reaction is to retire even more, redoubling her austerities. After a time, she and Giuliano move from her mother's to take up residence at his palazzo. She spends lonely winters there and lonely summers at his country place on the Riviera, about six miles from Genoa. Neglected by her husband, Catherine also feels abandoned by God.

In the succeeding five years, yielding to pressure from family and friends, she resumes social activities in keeping with her position in one of the leading families of Genoa. But she finds this a meaningless kind of existence and sinks deeper into despondency.

In mounting distress Catherine goes one day in March, 1474, to a nearby convent where her older sister Limbania is a nun. Limbania persuades her to talk to the chaplain. But hardly has she set foot in the chapel than the priest is momentarily called away.

Years later she will confide to her closest friend what happens in the short interval alone. As her friend describes it: "Her heart was pierced by so sudden and immense a love of God, accompanied by so penetrating a sight of her miseries and sins and of His goodness, that she was near falling to the ground. And in a transport of pure and all-purifying love, she was drawn away from the miseries of the world."

When the chaplain returns, Catherine can only manage to say, "Father, if you please, I should like to let this confession stand over to another time."

Overcome by the love God has revealed, she shuts herself up in her room for several days, during which time she has a vision of Christ. Following that, Catherine gives away all her fashionable clothes, makes a general confession, becomes a daily communicant—an extraordinarily rare practice then—and embarks on a lengthy penitential period. Always trying to be inconspicuous, she will walk a mile out of town to receive the Eucharist so that friends will not see her and wonder. From this instantaneous, total conversion of heart, Catherine will never once waver.

In the autumn of that same year Giuliano experiences a revelation of his own: the high cost of a dissipated life-style. He sells the country place and leases out the palazzo in town. A now remorseful husband confesses the existence of his natural daughter, Thobia. Apparently already knowing about her, Catherine assures him of her forgiveness.

Despite financial losses, sufficient income remains to live quite comfortably. Yet the two, at last in accord, decide instead to move into a little house in a neighborhood of working-class poor near the Hospital of the Pammatone. Both agree also to a life of chastity from then on. Giuliano joins the Third Order of St. Francis. Though Catherine feels strongly influenced by Franciscan teaching— particularly as expressed in the writings of mystic and poet Jacopone da Todi—she never shows an inclination to become a tertiary herself.

One day a friar tells her that he, as a religious, can love God better, chiding her for having "married the world." Catherine gets so wrought up over his remarks, her hair comes undone and falls about her shoulders as, face aflame, she bursts out: "If I thought your habit would enable me to love God better, I would tear it from your back!"

She has far from married the world. During the four years immediately following her conversion, she has spent six hours a day in prayer, coming from prayer "joyous and rosy-faced." As part of the fasting regime she continues for many years, she abstains from any solid food every Lent and Advent. Her friends marvel that during these fasting periods, Catherine is more active in pursuing good works, stronger and even more radiant than usual. It can only be explained as a special grace from God.

No longer does Catherine doubt the meaning of existence. She and Guiliano together attend to the needs of the sick and poor in their neighborhood in addition to caring for patients in the hospital. Giuliano has never worked at a previous occupation. The fastidious Catherine must overcome feelings of squeamishness when she cleans filth-ridden houses in the slum area and takes home for washing dirty, vermin-covered clothing.

In 1479 they move again, this time into two small rooms at the hospital, where both continue to perform even the most menial nursing chores, still at no pay. Catherine takes delight in singing lighthearted verses of her own composition in which she speaks to the Lord of love. Though she is a woman of powerful intellect and is generally viewed as rather sober-minded, the little rhymes reveal another facet of her nature:

> "Dost thou wish that I should show
> All God's Being thou mayst know?
> Peace is not found of those who do not with
>   Him go."

In the original Italian, the sound is melodious.

After 11 years of service, Catherine is appointed hospital matron, that is, director of the institution. When an epidemic of deadly fever strikes in the early spring of 1493 and lasts until the end of the summer, 80 percent of Genoa's citizens die. As matron, Catherine organizes medical staffing, supplemented by volunteer priests and tertiaries. To handle the overflow of patients, she has rows of sailcloth tents set up on the hospital's grounds. To her falls the task of bringing order out of a chaotic situation and easing the fears of panic-stricken victims. She is unsparing in her care for the sick.

Most who can afford to—that is, the wealthy class—flee the city while the epidemic rages. One who stays behind, Ettore Vernazza, a 23-year-old lawyer, enlists as an aide. When he and Catherine meet, it marks the start of a close, enduring friendship—though it very nearly misses being a long one. For in a compassionate gesture, she kisses a dying patient, contracts the disease and almost dies from the fever herself.

In 1496 Catherine's health begins to fail, marked primarily by great weakness of body. She therefore resigns her post as matron, although she still lives at the hospital and works when possible. A year later, after a long illness,

Giuliano dies. In his will he asks that Catherine see to the continued support of his daughter Thobia and the child's mother, as in the past. This Catherine takes care of with a characteristically generous spirit.

At this point her life takes a new turn. She suffers from an illness doctors can neither explain nor find treatment for (she speaks of "great burnings" on occasion). But Catherine recognizes it as nervous in origin. As the illness progresses and makes it impossible to work, she is free to spend much time with the circle of disciples who have been drawn to her and regard her as their spiritual mother.

Prominent among the men are Ettore Vernazza, along with Dom Cattaneo Marabotto, a priest appointed rector at the hospital around 1499. The latter becomes Catherine's spiritual director during these last years (until now, she has made her mystical pilgrimage on her own). His direction consists essentially in giving back to her, when asked, the words of counsel she gave him on some previous occasion.

Among her female disciples, a favorite is her cousin Tommasina. The two are the same age and share religious interests as well as intellectual pursuits. (The widowed Tommasina becomes first a Dominican tertiary, then a nun.) But they differ in personality. Tommasina likes to tease her more intensely tuned cousin, saying one day with a twinkle in her eyes, "What if, after all your mortifications, you decide it was all for naught?" Catherine's reply is a predictable, vehement, "Never!"

Tommasina, a gifted artist, is believed by some to have painted the portrait of Catherine which hangs in the Municipal Hospital of Genoa. The painting depicts its subject with a sensitive mouth but strong chin, oval face of delicate complexion, gray-blue eyes and thick dark hair.

Catherine has always been passionate about everything. In the final years the love that permeates Catherine's life encompasses God's other creations as well as humanity. Friends say that "if an animal were killed or a tree cut down, she could hardly bear to see them lose that being which God had given them."

She has the envied capacity to appreciate the sacrament

of the moment: finding God in the present, plumbing the depths of experience whether that be suffering, the commonplace or the sweetest peace. God, for Catherine—from moment of conversion to moment of death—is "Boundless Love."

Dom Marabotto and Ettore Vernazza team up to collect their spiritual mother's profound sayings and to record her life. Among her teachings, the treatise on purgatory presents one of the Church's most illuminating views on the subject—a classic in Catholic theology. Drawing from her own experience, Catherine interprets the way of purgation for the soul in this life or after death. She speaks of "the rust of sin which is the covering of the soul; in Purgatory the fire consumes it; the more it is consumed the more the soul reflects the true sun who is God." The joy of the soul, Catherine says, increases as the impediments to union with God are burned away. This treatise is only part of Catherine's larger doctrine on the all-embracing goodness of God, but it will be emphasized because of a controversy involving Martin Luther which happens shortly after her death in 1510.

In her last days Catherine tries to describe to her disciples exactly what mystical joy means. "Oh, would that I could tell you what my heart feels! I cannot find words appropriate to so great a love. But this I can say with truth, that if of what my heart feels one drop were to fall into hell, hell itself would turn into eternal life!"

AFTERWARD

Evelyn Underhill, a classic authority and writer on mysticism, described Catherine of Genoa as "one of the deepest gazers into the secrets of Eternal Love that the history of Christian mysticism contains."

This magnificent soul attained the summit of spirituality

in her own unique way—as a layperson independent of any affiliation—and even went without a spiritual director until the last years of her life. Like many other mystics, Catherine combined her full prayer life with one of active Christian charity.

Though her family tree included two popes (Innocent IV and Hadrian V) and one of her cousins was a prominent cardinal, she never showed a hint of interest in ecclesiastical affairs. Contrast the works of Genoa and the works of Rome: While Catherine was nursing plague victims and cleaning house for the sick poor of her city, popes of that era concentrated on the business of the Italian Renaissance, promoting the splendors of art and architecture. This occupied their energies to the extent that the murmurings of discontent across Christendom were either ignored or dismissed as being of no consequence.

In the quest for beauty one pope's papal crown cost two million francs. Another, Alexander VI (one of the notorious Borgias), added not only to the glory of Rome but to the bank accounts of his children and grandchildren as he distributed Church wealth among them. To pay for all the luxuries, indulgences as well as ecclesiastical offices were sold, and the murmurings grew to rumblings.

Still, the papacy neglected the conditions—indeed, aggravated them—which would lead to the Protestant Revolt soon after Catherine's death.

In her quiet way Catherine provided a needed spirituality for her time and, in her gospel kind of humanitarianism, she did "something beautiful for God."

The 16th Century

Teresa of Avila

BACKGROUND

When Martin Luther posted
his 95 theses on the church door in Wittenberg, it was not his
intention to challenge the structure of the entire Catholic
Church. Rather, he was just following normal procedure
among intellectuals wishing to debate an issue. Others had
been campaigning for reform before this Augustinian monk,
but circumstances made him the catalyst of the explosion of
unhappiness over the abuses and corruption in the Church.

It happened that Rome needed money again, this time to
help pay for the rebuilding of St. Peter's. Selling indulgences
promising a remission of punishment for sins to the faithful
of Europe offered a practical solution. Unfortunately for
Rome, nationalistic feelings were by now particularly strong
in Germany. Added to that, Germans had traditionally been
opposed to seeing their money go off to Rome. When Luther
made his protest against the sale of indulgences, a papal bull
condemned his views and ordered him to appear for a
hearing. He refused, perhaps afraid of being burned at the
stake as a heretic. When Luther sought political support
from German lords in the snowballing controversy, he
got it. German rulers and the papacy were not new to
confrontation. In 1521 Luther was excommunicated, even as
his movement grew to include far more reform issues than
the sale of indulgences.

In other countries, too, people were ready to revolt against papal authority. The English, for example, had long rebelled against Rome's interference in their internal politics. A dozen years after Luther's excommunication, Henry VIII lost his head over a woman capable of providing an heir to the throne; the papacy ruled against his remarriage and England set up its own Church, free to make its own rules.

Spain, however, was in a different mood. Only in 1492 had the last of the Moors (the Muslim presence) been thrown out of the country. All Jews were expelled too, and the land of the Iberian Peninsula was fully returned to Christian rule. For the Spanish there was no question that the Catholic Church was the sole answer to faith. The only question was: How exactly should that faith be lived?

AVILA, SPAIN, ALL SOULS' DAY 1536

In the chill November dawn Teresa de Ahumada steals away from the family home, a younger brother accompanying her as far as the gate of the Carmelite Convent of the Incarnation beyond the city walls. After five years of indecision, the young woman has settled on becoming a nun. She is making the move without her father's consent, though, and that causes her great distress.

It is not as if religious dedication were the motivating factor behind her choice. Rather, an illness brought Teresa to the realization that life could be cut short; because of her frivolous ways, hell might be her fate. In her autobiography she later admits to being "afraid of marriage" (perhaps the result of observing her mother's steady decline in health after a number of pregnancies). But fun-loving Teresa also views the cloister as a kind of purgatory, though she concludes that purgatory is preferable to hell. As she says: "I saw that this was the best and safest state, and so, little by little, I determined to force myself to embrace it."

The convent accepts 21-year-old Teresa, and the

following year she professes vows. Life at Incarnation is not without its compensations. Typical of religious communities then, visitors to the parlor, even gentlemen callers, are frequent—almost interminable, Teresa will eventually say—for the convent houses at least 130 nuns. Though some sleep in the dormitory, those who are well provided for by their families in terms of dowry enjoy private rooms. Because Teresa's father shortly comes around to her choice of vocation, she falls into the latter category. Those who can afford them feast on delicacies sent in, wear jewelry and make extended outside visits to family or friends.

A year after her profession, Teresa goes through a long period of illness marked by fainting fits and heart problems. When none of the doctors' ministrations help, she is sent for treatment to a *curandera* or female healer about 40 miles from Avila. Her condition worsens and, after a severe cataleptic fit that leaves her unconscious and unmoving for four days, a grave is even dug for her. (Catalepsy may be either neurological or psychological in origin. If the latter, the consequent paralysis is sometimes attributed to hysteria. Some scholars speculate that Teresa's illness was psychological in nature, prompted by interior struggles over her spiritual life.) Through the intercession of St. Joseph, as she believes, Teresa finally recovers sufficiently to return to the convent, though somewhat an invalid still. The effects of paralysis will stay with her for several years.

Beginning an attempt at serious prayer, she tries to find a confessor who will understand. Failing that, she turns for guidance to a book she read during the illness, Francisco de Osuna's *Third Spiritual Alphabet*. Osuna's words had made a strong impression upon her.

Although becoming increasingly aware of the shallowness of her interior life, Teresa remains torn between attempts at deeper prayer and the social distractions prevalent at the convent. She finds "neither any joy in God nor any pleasure in the world," she later reports. Her extroverted nature thrives on human company as well as its approval.

Her father's death in 1543 hits Teresa hard, for he was an

important figure in her life, a source of both comfort and support. (Her mother had died when she was 13.)

For a dozen years after that, she continues on the "stormy sea," as she calls it. One day, chancing to look at a picture of the wounded Christ, Teresa is struck by the realization of all he had suffered and "how ill I had repaid him for those wounds that I felt as if my heart were breaking." In "floods of tears," she begs Christ for the strength to change.

As the 40-year-old nun ponders how best to serve God, to make amends, the answer seems clear: Follow the vocation given her as perfectly as possible. But to fulfill that vow required a spiritually oriented environment. Unfortunately, the Convent of the Incarnation—like so many others—had drifted far from the original contemplative ideal of the Carmelite Order.

Teresa's dream, which she and a few others discuss, revolves around the idea of a handful of nuns living apart, austerely, with strict enclosure, according to the order's Primitive Rule.

Still the idea never gets beyond the talk stage until one day after communion when, Teresa relates, "the Lord gave me the most explicit commands to work for this aim," coupled with the promise that the convent she founds will "be a star giving out the most brilliant light." (She has already begun to experience visions.)

When she broaches the subject with the local provincial of the order, he is in favor of the proposal at first. But once word of it leaks out, the fireworks start. With only a few exceptions, the sisters at Incarnation ridicule Teresa when they are not accusing her of insulting them by implying that their convent is not good enough. Some even suggest she be thrown into the convent prison cell. (Such cells were then a common way to deal with problem nuns in a religious community.) Teresa's friends fear far worse, for a rumor has begun circulating about the nun's having revelations. Should the dreaded Spanish Inquisition, always on the hunt for false mystics as well as for heretics, hear of this, it will likely investigate her. Punishment entails prison, torture and sometimes death.

Yet even after the Carmelite nun's plan is denounced from the pulpits of Avila's churches—once, on an outing from the convent to visit family, she is in the congregation— she doggedly goes ahead with negotiations to purchase a small house for the envisaged new convent. The day before signing of the deed, however, the provincial withdraws his permission. He simply cannot deal with all the commotion.

Throughout the struggle to establish a reform convent, Teresa does get ongoing support from Peter of Alcantara, a Franciscan working to instill in his own order more contemplative and penitential practices. The two had first met when she was looking for guidance in understanding the intellectual visions she was beginning to receive. (As Teresa would explain this type of vision in subsequent writings, the person does not see the Lord with the eyes but "is conscious that Jesus Christ stands by her side....[A] most tender love for Him results from being constantly in His company, while the desire of devoting one's whole being to His service is more fervent than any hitherto described.")

As troubles mount, Peter, having gone through it himself, tells her that opposition from good people is one of the worst trials in the world. And sure enough, she suffers the greatest pain when the confessor now assigned to her chastises her for causing scandal, and orders no more talk or action regarding the project.

For the next five or six months, Teresa is in anguish— until an ecclesiastic new in authority proves to be on her side and directs the confessor to let the Spirit work through this crusading nun. To forestall the problems caused in the past by too much talk, it is agreed that henceforth the project must proceed in all secrecy.

Through her sister Juana, arrangements are made to buy and furnish a house. Funds provided by several donors, including a well-to-do widow, are not quite sufficient to pay the workmen hired to make the modest house fit to live in. This time her brother Lorenzo comes to the rescue. (Throughout her life, Teresa remains much involved in the welfare of her large family, as they do with her undertakings.)

The biggest worry now is that her provincial—one of those kept in the dark—will discover what's going on and put a stop to it. On the advice of Peter of Alcantara and a few others, steps are taken by way of friends in high places in Rome to put the new convent directly under the protection of Avila's bishop, who is an unwavering supporter of reform. Approval from Rome arrives in July 1562. The following month a handful of nuns sharing Teresa's outlook move into St. Joseph's, as it is named, and within days the sisters at Incarnation, along with all of Avila, hear the news. The prioress at Incarnation immediately sends for Teresa.

"I went in the belief that I should at once be put in prison," she admits. The provincial makes an appearance at the interview too. After Teresa goes through a careful explanation of how she is only trying to strengthen the order, they begin to see things her way.

Next to be placated are city officials, for they feel Avila already has more than its share of poor religious houses dependent on local support. A report is forwarded to the Royal Council, and Teresa is forbidden to move to St. Joseph's until the matter is settled legally. She cannot understand the commotion brought on by the thought of 12 poor women plus a superior in one little house. The nuns already in residence begin their life of contemplative prayer regardless of the uproar.

In a complete turnaround, the people of Avila, seeing that the opposition has not been able to halt the convent's opening, conclude it must be the work of God. Legal proceedings are forthwith dropped, and a wave of public generosity provides alms even without any need for an appeal.

Teresa is now free to join her little community, which she likens to heaven. No class distinctions exist at St. Joseph's. All share in the chores—Teresa included, for she firmly believes in a rhythm of work and prayer. The nuns wear coarse brown habits and hempen sandals. (They are called Discalced—that is, "barefooted"—Carmelites. Bare feet are a popular symbol of the day for the reform-minded, signifying poverty and simplicity.) But Teresa, who is always guided by good sense, makes sure her sisters have sandals.

Happier and healthier than ever before in the peacefulness of St. Joseph's, Teresa journeys to the heights of mystical prayer. Her superiors request that she write a spiritual autobiography, and after completing this, she begins work on an instructional book for prayer: *The Way of Perfection*.

In 1566 Teresa receives a promise from the Lord that soon she will "see great things." In April of the following year, the prior-general of the Carmelite Order arrives on visitation from Rome. In answer to the Protestant Reformation, bishops of the Church have come up with reforms of their own in a series of meetings (the Council of Trent, 1543-1563). The Carmelite head has come to Spain to make sure they are implemented. He likes what he sees at St. Joseph's and asks Teresa to do more of the same, giving her permission (although no money) to found not only more convents but also several reform houses for friars. She never worries about lack of funds but dives into the busiest period of her life.

While on a mission to Medina later that year, Teresa becomes acquainted with a brilliant, highly educated Carmelite friar known to history as John of the Cross. Despite the difference in age (she is 52 and he, 25), their rapport is immediate. She enlists John's help in working with men in the order. Their names will be forever linked as a result of their joint accomplishments. During the years of working closely together, the two obviously inspire each other, for each composes a masterpiece of literature: Teresa's *The Interior Castle* and John's *Spiritual Canticle*.

Their writing styles show the differences in their temperaments. She is witty and forceful; he is gentle and extremely sweet-natured. Her style is conversational, reflecting a natural exuberance, while his celebration of the love of God soars poetically.

When Teresa is recalled to Incarnation, John goes along as her confessor. This time, however, she will serve six years as prioress, there to reform the convent—a prospect which upsets some nuns at first. Even while in charge of her old community, the energetic nun manages to go on founding additional convents. And the pattern of establishing St. Joseph's keeps repeating itself: first, opposition; then, aided by Teresa's persistence as well as charm, people coming around to accepting the inevitable.

To keep up with all that's happening, she conducts a voluminous correspondence. "These letters are killing me," she tells a brother. Books are easier for her to do. By the light of an oil lamp, Teresa writes late at night, her only free time, her quill pen flying over the paper. Among her correspondents is Philip II, king of Spain, who likes her no-nonsense way. In this, Spain's "Golden Age," he is considered the most powerful man in Europe.

By 1577 the Carmelite reformer has become a national figure. The king's support for her is well known—she needs it when opponents report some of her writings to the Spanish Inquisition. An appeal to the king gets her out of trouble. John of the Cross is not so lucky. Friars twice kidnap and imprison him in Toledo, where they regularly flog him, before he manages to escape. Clergy and religious who resist change can be brutal as well as intolerant.

Teresa somehow keeps her famous sense of humor despite having her every move watched by persons who hope to catch her in a misstep. When one, for example, acts scandalized at seeing this nun of reforming zeal sit down to enjoy a meal of roast partridge prepared by the host, Teresa, never eccentric about religious practices, replies matter-of-factly: "There is a time for partridge and a time for penance."

Her extensive journeys to found convents continue to the very end. Sometimes the great distances of Spain are traversed by mule, more often in a covered mule-cart made without springs but with heavy wooden wheels for the rough, at times impassable, roads. Whether in summer heat or the ice, snow and floods of winter, she travels not only with sisters as companions but also with an escort of laymen plus two or three of the clergy because of the danger of brigands. The inns are squalid and crowded with adventurers.

On what is to be her final trip, Teresa, now 68, becomes

seriously ill at Alba de Tormes in the north-central part of the country. As death approaches, a priest asks if she would like her body returned to Avila for burial. "What?" she asks, still irrepressible. "Will they not give me a little earth here?"

AFTERWARD

The reawakening of religious fervor that Teresa set in motion in Spain spread soon after her death beyond Spain and across Christendom, with profound results for the Catholic Reformation. Because her country was then at the height of its power and wealth, what happened there tended to influence the course of the Church.

Teresa is regarded as one of the outstanding women in the history of Spain, and her books on the mystical life are valued as gems of Spanish literature as well as treasuries of spirituality.

Her spiritual friendship with John of the Cross is perhaps her most famous relationship, but she had a great capacity for friendship with both men and women. Her circle of admirers ever widened the older she got.

Women in Spain were constricted even more then than now, and so it is all the more remarkable how much she accomplished. (To be a woman at all, Teresa once remarked, was to feel your wings droop.)

A papal nuncio who referred to her as a "restless gadabout" complained, "She is ambitious and teaches theology as though she were a Doctor of the Church." Teresa had the last word—not surprisingly—for she became the first woman in the Church so designated.

Louise de Marillac

BACKGROUND

France was on its way to supplanting Spain as the dominant power in Europe. Cardinal Richelieu, the king's chief minister of state, pushed the advance through political and economic means. In France the Catholic Reformation had gotten off to a slow start because of the turmoil connected with intermittent religious wars on its soil, while elsewhere on the continent, Protestants and Catholics engaged in battles too. At one point, to keep Catholic Austria from becoming too powerful, Cardinal Richelieu arranged for the French to join forces with Protestant Sweden in a move against Austria.

In the meantime, reforms instituted by the Council of Trent in the mid-16th century had effected a sweeping housecleaning of abuses, and in the process turned the Church strongly in the direction of conservatism, not to reverse itself until Vatican II.

Women in religious life were more restricted in their activities than ever. In 17th-century France, though, women of the laity, particularly those of the upper classes, tended to have more educational opportunities and the chance to shine as individuals in society than they did in most European countries. From their ranks came some of the great names of contributors to the new spiritual vigor marking this period. Among them were individuals who aimed to live a Christian life in the world, although joining the Carmelites or other austere orders was also a popular choice. The first houses of reformed Carmelites had been set up in France in 1604, initially directed by nuns from Spain. Their contemplative spirituality had a significant influence on the French.

PARIS, FRANCE, JANUARY 1638

When Vincent de Paul learns from his friend Louise about the conditions at La Couche, he calls it "the shame of Paris."

Each year hundreds of babies born out of wedlock are being abandoned on church doorsteps and other public places by mothers too poor to keep them. State care is provided through a home called La Couche, operated by an appointed matron who is aided by two hired servants. To quiet the crying infants, the women administer laudanum (an opium preparation). Some babies are sold to practitioners of black magic and devil worship and used as ritual victims. Others are bought by professional beggars who break the babies' bones before employing them as props to arouse pity as the beggars ply their trade.

Something must be done to remedy this horror, Monsieur Vincent declares. Agreeing wholeheartedly, Louise begins, as she does with every undertaking, by drawing up guidelines. Experience tells her that building the right organization is the most critical phase.

Initially, arrangements are made to remove 12 infants from the infamous La Couche, to be cared for instead by staff from her own community of young women devoted to helping the poor. In addition, she employs wet nurses; a mother herself, Louise knows the nutritional importance of breast-feeding, particularly for babies whose start in life has been so precarious. This model project grows so that within five years more than 1200 infants will have been cared for.

Of all the varied ministries Louise engages in, the ones

associated with the welfare of children remain closest to her heart. Surely the loneliness she experienced as a child has something to do with it.

Her father, Louis de Marillac, was of distinguished family, and two of his brothers held high positions at the royal court. She was born during the period between her father's two marriages and never knew who her mother was. Her father acknowledged her as his natural daughter, providing for her upbringing, but she was never part of the family when he entered into a second, quite unhappy marriage with a widow who had four children.

At an early age, she was placed in the care of an aunt who was a nun at a prestigious Dominican convent, and there the girl received an excellent classical education. She was 13 when her father died. It was a great blow to her. After that, her education took a more practical turn, for she boarded with a woman who taught her sewing, cooking and household management. Eager at the time to enter a religious order, Louise was turned down because of delicate health. That left only one alternative—marriage. Thus came about her union with Antoine le Gras, secretary to the Queen Regent, Marie de Medici.

When the marriage bans were proclaimed, Louise's status at birth became public knowledge—certainly a humiliation for her, since her husband's position entailed socializing with the nobility. The marriage, nevertheless, proved a happy one, and the birth of a son within a year was an occasion for rejoicing.

Along with her household and social obligations, Louise managed to fit in charitable work for her parish church. Despite this full life, she became at times quite introspective about her early desire to be a nun, feeling guilty that she had not been able to follow through. Spiritual directors advised her not to think about it. These episodes of melancholy may have been triggered by the strain of nursing her husband, whose health was on the wane.

After a prolonged illness, Antoine died in 1625, leaving Louise, at age 34, with their 12-year-old son Michel. Though Antoine had made provisions to insure her an income, still she had to adjust to one reduced in scale.

She moved to a smaller house on the Rue Saint Victor, near Notre Dame, because that is the district where Michel went to school and where her spiritual director for the past year or two, Vincent de Paul, headquartered his company of mission priests. ("Monsieur" Vincent—as priests were addressed then—had not been eager to act as her director, yet gave in to pressure from a bishop friend. Louise, incidentally, was known as "Mademoiselle" le Gras. In 17th-century France only ladies of the high nobility were addressed as "Madame." After her husband's death, she resumed her maiden name, as was customary in France when the husband was of inferior rank.)

Louise continued her parish work of serving the poor, for she believed love of God is best shown in love of neighbor. She longed to make a more permanent kind of commitment, but Monsieur Vincent put her off. He characteristically waited until God's will was clear to him before taking any action.

In early May, 1629, her prayer was answered at last. Vincent sent a note explaining that he had been asked to give a mission outside of Paris and must leave at once, adding that there was work for her, too, at this place called Montmirail if she finds the idea agreeable. "Does your heart tell you to come there, Mademoiselle?" Vincent wrote. Knowing very well what her response would be, he added instructions on which coach to take.

Louise's assignment in Montmirail was to spend some time reviewing the local "Charity." This was a volunteer group comprised of laypersons, primarily women, who served the sick and poor of their parish. Vincent had started the first such Charity when he was briefly a pastor in a rural parish more than 20 years before. (He was of peasant background himself.) After founding his order, the Congregation of the Mission, dedicated to preaching as well as works of mercy in Paris and elsewhere, he and his priests continued the practice of setting up local lay confraternities to attend to needs on a permanent basis. With the passage of time, some Charities lost their fervor, and others needed to be taught newer methods of dealing with problems related to poverty.

After Louise met with unqualified success in reinvigorating the Montmirail group, Vincent came to rely on her for visitations to other Charities. A delicate constitution did not hinder her from arduous journeys on public stage coaches. She stayed at the cheapest inns, for she wanted to be one with the poor. Her baggage was filled chiefly with medical supplies for parish confraternities. (Years of nursing her husband had given Louise a considerable knowledge of medicine.)

On arriving in a country parish, she would impress the lay volunteers by her manner of instructing them through example, not just words, as this clearly cultured woman went into the rude hovels typical of the village poor to clean, cook and tend the sick.

On one of the early visitations, Louise became acquainted with a cowherd, 17-year-old Marguerite Naseau, who was so determined to learn that she had taught herself to read. Then, in an eagerness to share, she had begun teaching others. This struck a responsive chord, for Louise too sought to promote education, especially for girls, seeing it as a way of overcoming their lack of opportunity. When she talked with Vincent about Marguerite's desire to come to Paris and work among the poor, they concluded that the vocation was a true one. Marguerite thus became the first young woman of peasant stock to lodge in Louise's home. More would follow.

Louise's "Little Company" evolved at just the right moment. For, though Vincent had established parish charities in Paris, many of the women with the luxury of time to volunteer came from aristocratic backgrounds. They consequently knew scarcely anything about performing the menial domestic chores necessary in caring for the sick poor. And even among those willing to try, many had husbands understandably alarmed about their wives going into the often vermin-infested houses of the poor.

Women from the villages, on the other hand, were accustomed to hard labor, in addition to being free of the social strictures that go with an upper-class standing. (When some of the latter sent their servants to do the work for them, Vincent and Louise objected, since the whole point was to give of themselves.)

At the prompting of a close friend of Louise, a number of the highborn banded into a citywide association called Ladies of Charity, serving the poor directly when their husbands permitted and providing financial support for works of mercy. But the work itself fell increasingly on the shoulders of Louise's Little Company.

When she wanted to formalize her group—never having given up wanting to be a nun—Vincent resisted. He had seen what happened when his friend, Bishop Francis de Sales, cofounded with Jeanne d'Chantal the Order of Visitation, intending that the sisters serve the world. The Church decreed that congregations of women must be cloistered, and the Visitation nuns unhappily took that state. The Daughters of Charity *must* be free to serve. Vincent insisted on that.

A solution was in the making, however. On November 29, 1633, a red-letter day for Louise, four young women agreed to live a common life in her home as laypersons, not nuns. Some months later, with 11 under her direction, Louise presented them with a rule of life she had worked out; it stressed at least an hour each day for prayer. (The problem of vows will eventually be circumvented when Vincent arranges for the Daughters of Charity to renew their promises on an annual basis rather than taking permanent vows as traditional orders do. This will seem to satisfy ecclesiastical authorities.)

Although, in the early years, theirs was not officially a religious congregation, the public regarded the women as nuns. They wore ordinary dress—modest gray gowns and white kerchief headcoverings—but were easily identifiable by their uniform attire. People reacted with shock at the idea of nuns freely going about city streets to work among the poor. When her Daughters were subject to taunts and sometimes stone-throwing, Louise consoled them: "A little patience, my Sisters, all these are only clouds which prevent you for a time from seeing how sweet God is to those who wish to love and serve Him."

Aided by her guidelines—abetted by her organizational ability—the Daughters soon earn respect for a range of ministries. They bring, for instance, a progressive approach to nursing at Hotel Dieu, the mammoth hospital of Paris. So little does the hired staff know about even elementary hygiene that a mother with a new baby may be placed next to a patient with smallpox; the overcrowding is such that at times a bed meant for two ends up with six occupants. The Daughters' reputation for competence results in their being the first women sent to the battlefield to nurse wounded soldiers at Sedan, in 1641.

France's involvement in the Thirty Years' War (1618-1648) and civil war, too, makes for unsettled conditions. An estimated 40,000 beggars roam the streets of Paris. At three sites in the city, Louise and her sisters coordinate soup kitchens, serving 7,000 meals daily. War refugees must be cared for, and free schools teaching occupational skills opened for poor girls in both the war-torn provinces and Paris. Louise develops as a pilot project the first hospice for the elderly, providing workrooms where they can feel useful by employing their talents to make saleable items. The commissions give them pocket money, which the men tend to spend on wine.

Vincent asks Louise to train some of her Daughters for nursing work in the prisons, where conditions reduce many of the convicts to the level of beasts. "It is a challenge for your adventurous mind," he tells her. Though not naive about the possibilities of danger, she instructs the sisters to pray and behave with modesty and God will keep them from harm. No harm befalls any of them.

Louise still finds time to worry about her son Michel, who lacks the capabilities she likes to think he possesses. Vincent chides her, "I have never seen a mother who was so much a mother as you are." Michel goes on to marry and lead a good and normal life.

Vincent, in turn, fusses over Louise's welfare, giving her such homely advice as "eat eggs" when she is ill and insisting she not fast during Lent since she needs her strength for her social work.

He leans on her too, writing at one time, in reference to some troubles he's been having, "all this is confided to your heart alone, and no other." On another occasion he confesses: "God alone knows, Mademoiselle, what He has done for me in giving you to me. In heaven you will know." Their exchange of notes and letters when apart provides history with a wealth of information.

These two noble hearts, after long lives of service, pass from this earth within six months of each other.

AFTERWARD

The Daughters of Charity were the first community of women since the early Church who did not live a cloistered or contemplative life. Louise liked to say she contemplated Christ in the poor. She drew her original vocations from among peasant women who would otherwise have gone into domestic service or become farm laborers. In the process she and Vincent created a revolutionary form of religious community, unleashing a power latent in women to overwhelm the world with monumental good works. At the time of her death in 1660, there were already more than 40 houses of her sisters. Today the Daughters of Charity number more than 30,000 on five continents.

In almost as radical a move, Vincent had her conduct retreats (women did not do this) for ladies of nobility while he did so for the men, saying that they needed spiritual nourishment as much as the poor needed their soup kitchens.

Louise and Vincent together pioneered in all aspects of social service. Space limits describing all their "firsts." They of course paved the way for all the other congregations who engage in social work and teaching.

Anne Marie Javouhey

BACKGROUND

An intellectual revolution
paved the way for the French Revolution—much of it carried
on in cosmopolitan salons presided over by aristocratic
Frenchwomen of 18th-century Paris. Long before, however,
the Renaissance which exalted human accomplishments had
initiated the movement toward the modern, secular age. The
Renaissance was followed by revolt against an authoritarian
Church at Rome. Then the exploration of new lands around
the globe opened European minds to wider horizons.
Finally, the Age of Enlightenment, centered in 18th-century
France, extolled human reason to the extent that it became a
god in place of God. Institutional religion was downgraded
when not ignored outright by the intellectuals.

During Louis XIV's 70-year reign (ending in 1715),
France came to be Europe's wealthiest country—and
undoubtedly its most extravagant. There was a steady drain
on the state treasury to pay for French involvement in a
succession of wars (including financial support for the
American Revolution), in addition to the high cost of the
luxury-loving royal court at Versailles. This made necessary
a crushing burden of taxation levied on the lower classes
while the nobility and higher clergy escaped taxation.

People's attitude toward parish priests was usually
benign, for the lower clergy were often as impoverished as

the peasants to whom they ministered. But the resentment the poor directed at the nobility and the higher clergy grew stronger. The situation could not continue. With an angry mob's storming of the Bastille in 1789, the traditional social and political order broke down completely.

VILLAGE OF CHAMBLANC, FRANCE, 1797

Hearing shouts and pounding on the front door after dark, the Javouhey family and their guest—an outlawed priest—are paralyzed by fear. All but 17-year-old Nanette; she urges the priest to duck into the closet, then coolly opens the front door to greet four men. One is the local deputy for the revolutionary government. "Where's the priest?" he demands.

Nanette laughs as she denies they are harboring a priest. She asks for their coats and moves to hang them in the closet, meanwhile reminding her father he should get their company a glass of wine. The men decline the offer, retrieve their coats and go on their way, anxious to track down the fugitive priest they are sure is hiding somewhere in the neighborhood. If caught, he'll likely be executed.

This is only one of a number of times that Nanette keeps her head—while risking her life—to safeguard a priest. When the revolution in France had begun almost a decade before, its leaders waged war against the Church in violent reaction to the years in which many in the hierarchy lived in luxury, associating with the nobility, while the majority of the people as well as the lower clergy suffered poverty. Church lands were confiscated and religious institutions closed. Priests who refused to take a civil oath—in effect, becoming a branch of the civil service—were treated as criminals. When the Reign of Terror broke out in 1793, thousands of priests and nuns went to the guillotine or were condemned to prisons in French Guiana, such as the infamous Devil's Island. Priests who escaped capture but did not flee abroad joined an underground network to serve devout Catholics who were forced to practice their faith secretly—like those in the village where Nanette and her family lived.

Growing up in these times so terrifying for religious people, Nanette wants still to be a nun. She creates a sanctuary in a corner of the garden for daily prayer and, despite her youth, teaches the forbidden catechism to the children of Chamblanc under cover of her father's barn.

Even if convents were open to postulants, Balthazar Javouhey would object. He wants his favorite daughter to marry a farmer and settle down to a normal life. Their disagreement over her future reaches the stage in which, at times, she sends him letters via a younger sister rather than argue face-to-face. Nanette keeps hoping the political situation will change. And with Napoleon's takeover of the government in 1801, the Church's fortunes do improve markedly. Napoleon makes peace with the pope and allows the reopening of religious houses. It is a wise move, for the country needs all the help possible to repair the havoc wrought by the revolution. No institution can equal the Church for making human resources available for education and social services.

In this welcome new freedom, Nanette goes away to convents for two brief periods, but neither one seems the right place for her despite the strong attraction she has to the vocation itself.

Her mother Claudine, a woman of great piety, seems only to shrug when her husband gets riled. While Balthazar does not understand Nanette and wishes fervently that she would come to her senses, he unfailingly supports her endeavors—as when, after her first convent experience, Nanette seeks to open a school in a neighboring village. In less than a year she returns home in failure. The next venture in a village 30 miles away also ends in failure. Financial assistance promised by village priests does not materialize owing to their own poverty. Lacking help with the work and without funds, she must go back to her family again.

The priest advising her suggests a Trappistine convent

for training in spiritual practices to serve as her bulwark. After Nanette spends a few tranquil months there, he counsels that she must again resume the active life.

Her third attempt at trying to run a school for orphans proves the most disastrous experiment of all. At one point food for the children entrusted to her runs out. A woebegone Nanette goes to pray at a nearby chapel. Knocking on the tabernacle door, she cries, "I need help! Please, please help!" In answer, a voice says, "Have you no faith in me?" Then it tells her to return to the orphanage. She runs back to see her father and brother Pierre just arriving in a cart loaded with food.

Nevertheless, this proves but a stopgap measure, and she must return to Chamblanc, where her father—throwing up his hands in despair—boards off half the family home as a convent. For it seems that Nanette's three younger sisters want to be nuns too, teaching nuns.

Balthazar builds a small schoolhouse on his property. He also transports back to Chamblanc the orphans from the last failed school to become the first pupils in this new enterprise. When neighbors ask who the youngsters arriving in his cart are, Balthazar proudly replies, "These are my daughter's children."

When Pope Pius VII, on a tour through France, schedules a visit to the town of Chalon, 75 miles from her home, Nanette decides to join the welcoming throngs. She finds herself granted a few minutes to speak with the pope, and when she tells him of her work in teaching the faith, he warmly approves. This spurs her to accept an offer to run a parish school in Chalon. Seeing the excellent results achieved by the young woman, the pastor encourages her to think of starting her own congregation.

Good fortune continues to shine for the moment on Nanette, as the government makes available an unused seminary outside of Chalon, with facilities to accommodate 125 students. Here she and the eight now on her teaching staff, including her three sisters, model their life on that of a religious community. The schools at Chamblanc and Chalon still operate under their auspices. Nanette takes to signing her letters home as "Sister Anne Marie." (Anne Marie was her baptismal name; Nanette is the family's pet name for her.)

At age 27, she officially becomes Sister Anne Marie, for her congregation, with herself as superior, gets approval from the requisite episcopal and government authorities. The small band of teaching sisters intends to conduct schools and orphanages, with emphasis on educating the poor. There are plans also to aid the sick and aged.

Several years later the government reclaims the seminary, saying the group was granted its use only temporarily. Once more Balthazar Javouhey comes to the rescue, in 1812 buying the little community both house and property at Cluny, a place rich in history as the center of Church reform in the Middle Ages. Henceforth, the congregation will call itself the Sisters of St. Joseph of Cluny. This puts the motherhouse in the diocese of Autun, therefore coming under obedience to its bishop, a circumstance which will cause no end of trouble in Anne Marie's future. But for the moment she is concerned with the congregation's rapid expansion. With a flood of applicants, new convents must be set up.

Part of the expansion includes opening a school in Paris, where Anne Marie inaugurates a controversial but highly successful system of education. Known as the Lancaster system after its developer, English educator Joseph Lancaster, it makes use of the older, brighter students in a school as teaching assistants. This enables a limited professional staff to teach larger numbers with greater effectiveness. The method soon proves a boon to mass education for the poor. A major point of controversy is the system's origin in England, a traditional enemy of France.

Anne Marie consequently enjoys a reputation as one of the country's leading educators, drawing attention and a visit from the governor of a French colony in the Indian Ocean, off the eastern coast of Africa. He asks for teaching nuns, and when Anne Marie discovers that most of the children in the colony of Bourbon (known today as Reunion) are black, there is no question but that she will dispatch sisters to implement her new system of education. Years before, though she was not then aware of people whose color was other than white, she had a vision of many dark-skinned boys and girls, along with a woman who identified herself as Teresa of Avila and said, "These are the children that God is giving you." The vision had occurred at a time when Anne Marie was praying to know God's will for her life.

She longs to go with the four sisters assigned to the island of Bourbon, but her first consideration must be to figure out ways of financing the new schools which the congregation is opening throughout France.

The work at Bourbon, meanwhile, progresses exceedingly well. Government authorities are so pleased that they request Sisters of St. Joseph for colonies in the West Indies, South America and Senegal. The latter, on Africa's west coast, is France's oldest and most neglected colony.

Anne Marie appoints her youngest sister, Rosalie, to be in charge of a small group of nuns at the Senegal mission. Once settled there, Rosalie writes back: "Were I to describe to you what I have witnessed and learned of the habits and customs of this savage country you would not read my account of it a second time, but rather close your eyes to it and pray that God in His mercy would enlighten the darkness and ignorance of these unhappy people. It will take years to train them, but our Sisters are indefatigable." As culturally insensitive as Rosalie's remarks are, she reflects the general thinking of her day among missionaries. Anne Marie will pursue a different course.

Anne Marie feels compelled to see for herself. At first opportunity, with affairs running smoothly in France, she impulsively sets off for the colony early in 1822 to spend several years as a missionary. Like the other nuns, she will nurse rather than teach, for that is the critical need in Senegal. Anne Marie also encounters the problem of slavery. Seeing a 10-year-old girl about to be consigned to service, she buys the girl for 300 francs, and Florence is from then on her steady companion.

When Anne Marie at last returns to France with Florence in tow, she is heartsick to learn the extent of troubles fomented by one of her own nuns in the Bourbon colony. A Sister Thais, looking to take over as superior there in every respect even though Anne Marie had named someone else to the post, has manipulated the officials and priests in the colony and even the nuns, so that all believe she is but a meek and pious nun being much abused by congregation headquarters in France. Because of the distances involved (a ship's journey, carrying mail or replacement nuns, takes up to six months), it requires several years' effort to untangle Sister Thais's web of deceit. Anne Marie is finally obliged to work through friends at the royal court before the government ministry with the final say on the colonies orders Thais and her band of rebel sisters back to France. None, of course, remains with the Cluny congregation.

When the government requests teachers and nurses for the South American colony of Guiana, Anne Marie at age 50 leads the contingent from Cluny. While so far from home, she learns of her father's death. Balthazar, ever supportive, had been looking after her brother Pierre's wife and children so that Pierre could lend aid to Anne Marie in bringing order to the new mission. In the period before she left for Guiana, her mother had died, as well as Anne Marie's adopted daughter Florence, whose health had failed under the strain of the adjustment from African to French climate.

When Anne Marie has black children attend school alongside the French children in Guiana, her popularity with the French settlers plummets. In fact, they resist any attempts she makes to improve the lot of the natives.

After five years in the colony, she returns to Paris, where a government commission has requested her help in organizing a model project for freed slaves in Guiana. The government has passed a bill to free them after a seven-year probationary period in which slaves are expected to prove themselves capable of being self-sufficient. Details to implement the bill need to be worked out. Though ready to assume charge of the project, Anne Marie must first deal with trouble in her own backyard again.

This time it comes from the new bishop of the Autun diocese, where the Cluny motherhouse is located. Bishop d'Hericourt is of the old school, determined to assert his episcopal authority over the woman he regards as an upstart. It marks the beginning of an 18-year war between the two, with the bishop using every means at his disposal (including high-placed friends in the Church) to make life difficult for her. At one point, he even accuses the Cluny nuns of wearing an "indecent" guimpe (the white collar rimming their blue habits). D'Hericourt threatens to withhold the permission she needs in order to leave the diocese for the mission in South America. Thus she is forced to sign an agreement granting him the final say in running her order.

Finally able to leave for French Guiana, she stops long enough in Senegal to pick up 60 African women who are in the market for husbands. (Most of the 600 slaves she will be working with are male.) Once in Guiana, she organizes a settlement in a district called Mana to initiate her project. Despite opposition from colonial plantation owners, who see their free labor lost forever and economic competition besides, Mana flourishes. Having grown up a farm girl, Anne Marie knows the skills necessary to survive in an agricultural community. But part of the success is owed to her guidance in setting up a distillery, using the abundant sugar cane raised to produce rum for an eager French market.

Ignoring—and sometimes escaping—threats to her life, Anne Marie further wins the favor of her slaves-on-probation when she walks 50 miles through jungle to report the murder of one to the colonial administration. A plantation owner trying to reclaim his former slaves from Mana had burned one of them alive.

Although thousands of miles away, Bishop d'Hericourt gets back into the picture by allying himself with the plantation owners. He also has the local bishop excommunicate Anne Marie because she refuses to sign another document sent from Autun, this one allowing D'Hericourt to remake the Cluny constitution. Being deprived of the Eucharist causes her enormous spiritual suffering. She carries on, nevertheless, with her government assignment, departing Mana only when the slaves have proved self-sufficiency and are assured their freedom. When the Mana colony receives the vote, they want Anne Marie as their delegate to the French parliament and are disappointed that she cannot be. She tells others that Mana has been the place of her greatest happiness.

In Paris again, Anne Marie is able to find a friendly bishop who reinstates her in the good graces of the Church. D'Hericourt still continues to interfere with Cluny, but the Revolution of 1848 prevents her from going to Rome to appeal. During the brief but violent revolution the archbishop of Paris, who has been backing D'Hericourt, is killed while trying to cross a barricade in the city. (Just the night before, Anne Marie, recognized by a guard manning the same barricade, was allowed to pass through without question.) A new archbishop arranges for the motherhouse to be moved to Paris permanently—out of D'Hericourt's reach. Having already won freedom for the slaves, Anne Marie wins freedom for her congregation too.

AFTERWARD

At her death two years later, at age 71, Anne Marie's order had 118 houses, with 700 sisters in France and 300 more in Africa, South America, India and Tahiti.

In testimony to her accomplishments a government proclamation was issued in praise of Sister Anne Marie. King Louis Philippe (with whom she was in great favor) once said to friends, "Take my word for it. Madame Javouhey is a great man!"

In the 19th-century Church France was to take the leading role in supplying missionaries to work with people of color in the Third World. The same year that Anne Marie embarked on her first missionary journey to Senegal, 1822, Pauline Jaricot, a 23-year-old woman in Lyons, France, was organizing the missionary aid society which was destined to grow into the Society for the Propagation of the Faith.

Years ahead of her time, Anne Marie became more and more convinced of the need for a native clergy, but others did not support the idea.

Her congregation today remains international in scope, with many convents throughout the world. It engages in all kinds of work, depending on the needs of the particular area: teaching, pastoral ministry in parishes and in hospitals, religious education, nursing, rural ministry.

Elizabeth Lange

BACKGROUND

Maryland became a colony in 1634 under the aegis of an English-born Catholic, Lord Baltimore. Freedom was guaranteed for all religions, making Maryland attractive to Protestant settlers as well as Catholics; they soon outnumbered the Catholic population. After that, Catholics were relegated to second-class status and not even allowed to vote until after the Revolutionary War, when they proved their patriotism to the satisfaction of Protestant Americans (at least for the moment).

In 1784 a priest named John Carroll (cousin to Charles Carroll, a signer of the Declaration of Independence) was appointed by the Vatican as "Superior of the Mission in the thirteen United States." (Before that, the overseer was in London.) A few years later, Carroll became Bishop of Baltimore. The original diocese extended north to Maine, south to Georgia and west to the Mississippi River. Catholics in this territory numbered about 35,000; the bulk of them lived in Maryland and Pennsylvania. In all the United States at this time, less than 10 percent of the population professed membership in any denomination.

The Baltimore see was soon divided into smaller dioceses and additional bishops named. In the beginning they were elected by the American clergy, with papal approval following; the Mass was even said in English. But such

democratic tendencies were soon reversed. As a priest
Carroll had pushed for democracy; as archbishop and head
of the Church in the United States, he opted for control from
the top down.

Maryland was a natural hub of American Catholic life.
One of the first seminaries was opened in Baltimore just
prior to the 19th century. Shortly after, the first parochial
school was established in Emmitsburg, Maryland, by
Elizabeth Seton, who also founded the first American
religious order of nuns.

Black Catholics, however, need not apply for seminary,
school or convent. In fact, religious orders as well as
individual Catholic laypeople continued to own slaves, and
the Church never did play a significant role in the later
campaign to free them.

BALTIMORE, MARYLAND, OCTOBER 1847

On his knees, the young
priest begs the archbishop, "Most Reverend Father, only
give me your blessing, with your permission on trial."

Until now Archbishop Eccleston has seen no point in
providing support—moral or financial—for the Oblate
Sisters of Providence. In fact, in the past he has suggested
that the congregation disband, and his opinion is also shared
by many in the Catholic community, both clergy and laity.
But when Father Thaddeus Anwander, a Redemptorist
priest from Germany, learned of the nuns' desperate
situation, he told his superior, who then sent him to the
archbishop.

Anwander hopes to be assigned the pastoral care of the
sisters, but first Archbishop Eccleston must approve it. The
humility with which the priest pleads his case wins over the
archbishop, and that same day, Father Anwander hurries to
the Oblate house to give the nuns the good news. He
promises them the kind of help that got the order started.

The story actually begins about 30 years before, with the arrival in Baltimore of Elizabeth Lange, a refugee born in Cuba of San Domingan parents. (Her father may have been white; her mother was black. In any case, Elizabeth is considered "colored.") The Maryland city had earlier become a haven for French Catholics fleeing revolution in their country. The upheaval, felt as far away as France's colonies in the Caribbean, precipitated another wave of refugees, attracted to Baltimore by the existence of a large French-speaking community.

Haven notwithstanding, Maryland is also a slave-holding state where harsh discrimination against people of color is common and education for blacks almost nonexistent. Disturbed by what she encounters, Elizabeth, who is well educated herself, feels called to do what she can.

She has a small income, possibly from her father in Cuba. (Shy and reserved, Elizabeth will say little of her life previous to the Baltimore period.) With the aid of another refugee, Marie Balas, she organizes a free school for black children in her home.

Ministry to San Domingan Catholics—both white and black—has become a special province of Sulpician priests, in addition to their operation of St. Mary's Seminary in Baltimore. (Sulpicians were also refugees of French background.) At the seminary chapel, which also serves as a parish church, whites worship on the upper floor while Catholics of color celebrate their Mass in the basement.

When Father James Joubert is named chaplain for the black congregation, he discovers that many of the children in his catechism class cannot read the lessons. While outlining a plan to open a school for them, he learns that Elizabeth and several other women in the congregation have been running a small free school at home for 10 years but, because of insufficient funds, it is in danger of being discontinued.

Joubert meets Elizabeth, and they discuss the possibility of working together. Impressed with the commitment she shows to her faith, he promises his backing if she will form a religious community of black women to provide a teaching base, for, at that time, no order allowed blacks to enter. As part of the arrangement, Joubert is expected to keep the accounts, and Elizabeth will regulate community life and oversee instruction.

Joubert is successful in acquiring funds from several affluent whites originally from San Domingo. Subsequently, a house is rented—large enough to accommodate 11 boarders and nine day students paying tuition, along with four orphan girls admitted free.

Father Joubert approaches the new Archbishop Whitfield to gain approval for the initial phase of Elizabeth Lange's religious community. (She has quickly found three others willing to join.) The man Whitfield just replaced had voiced some objections but, to Joubert's relief, the new archbishop warmly welcomes the proposal.

The four aspiring nuns move into the schoolhouse to begin their year's novitiate while also teaching. Before the year is over, their landlord gives notice, saying he has other plans for the property. A bit of difficulty is encountered in renting another place the moment an owner discovers the prospective tenants' color. But eventually a white doctor of San Domingan origin comes to their aid and makes a house available at affordable cost.

On July 2, 1829, the women pronounce vows—the first black women ever formed into their own religious community. According to their Rule: "The Oblate Sisters of Providence are a Religious Society of virgins and widows of color. Their end is to consecrate themselves to God in a special manner not only to sanctify themselves and thereby secure the glory of God, but also to work for the Christian education of colored children." Elizabeth Lange takes the name Sister Mary.

They adopt a habit consisting of a black dress, cape and bonnet. (Indoors, the bonnet is replaced by a white cap banded with a black ribbon.) In his diary Father Joubert tells of the women's feelings of discouragement over public reaction to black women in habits. Nuns in general were quite accustomed to being pelted with mud or stones as well as subjected to verbal insults, for America's Catholic minority was often discriminated against. But Elizabeth

Lange, now Sister Mary, and her companions also have to
endure the same treatment from white Catholics. Joubert
admits to his diary of hearing from white parishioners who
"could not think of the idea of seeing these poor girls
(colored girls) wearing the religious habit and constituting a
religious community." And some members of the clergy tell
him that blacks have "neither souls to be saved nor minds to
be instructed."

He presents the situation to the archbishop, who replies,
"Monsieur Joubert, it is not lightly but with reflection that I
approved your project. I knew and saw the finger of God.
Besides, have I not the power to make foundations in my
diocese, in my episcopal city, of any religious establishment
whatever?"

That settled, the archbishop promises to protect the new
foundation. Joubert relays his message to the nuns. Thus
bolstered, they persevere. Sister Mary would later say of
Joubert: "He was the greatest friend the Oblates ever had."

About herself she speaks little, though community
annals note of this petite yet physically strong—and strong-
willed—woman: "If there was work to be done, she was the
first to volunteer."

When a cholera epidemic strikes the city in 1832, Sister
Mary is among the four Oblates who spend a month caring
for patients in the city's almshouse, staying until the worst is
over. In the appeal for help, the Baltimore Bureau of the Poor
had originally asked the Sisters of Charity (the congregation
founded by Elizabeth Seton) for eight nuns. That order was
able to spare only half the number, so the Oblates stepped in.
(All 11 sisters offered to serve. The Baltimore City Council
later issued a resolution publicly thanking the Sisters of
Charity but making no mention of the Oblates.)

The order suffers its first loss because of the epidemic.
The nun who had earlier nursed the archbishop back to
health after his bout with cholera succumbs to the disease
herself while caring for Whitfield's stricken housekeeper.
Burial is in the Cathedral cemetery, in the section set apart
for the colored.

When the epidemic subsides, the nuns resume their

teaching duties. The only blight on their days comes from continuing complaints by white neighbors of their presence. But this is offset by Whitfield's unflagging support, along with the happiness engendered by Rome's approval of their congregation.

Because their residence is some distance from St. Mary's Seminary, the archbishop gives permission for the Blessed Sacrament to be reserved in the convent chapel. (The diary of one of the sisters says of Sister Mary: "The Blessed Sacrament was always her refuge.") Father Joubert's diary makes note of a feast-day Mass in the chapel served for the first time by two of the students, with a third carrying the censor: "These were girls."

To obtain more pupils, the nuns place an advertisement in the 1835 *United States Catholic Almanac,* explaining that the Oblates offer "A School for Colored Girls." The school's prospectus, presumably prepared by Father Joubert, lists the subjects taught: reading, writing, French, English, arithmetic, all kinds of fine sewing, embroidery, bead work and gold work, geography, music, washing and ironing (the last two no doubt because most students are expected to "become mothers of families or domestic servants").

Life at the school is close-knit for teachers and children, whether they are praying the rosary together at noon or sharing the midday meal. At the end of the school day, while the boarding students study or enjoy recreation, the nuns sew as an income-producing activity, including vestments for the seminary.

The community continues to grow in the number of both sisters and pupils. One other addition, in 1836, is Sister Mary's elderly mother, who comes from Cuba after the death of her husband. He has left an estate amounting to $1,411.59, which is contributed to the Oblates. (Sister Mary had already donated the major part of her assets at the time the order was founded.)

The Oblates' relatively peaceful existence changes abruptly with the death of Father Joubert in 1843 and that of Archbishop Whitfield a year later. Many former supporters cease helping. Direct diocesan funding had never been available, though Whitfield's endorsement in the past encouraged some benefactors. When Joubert's superior at the seminary asks support for the Oblates' work from the new archbishop, Samuel Eccleston, the latter reportedly replied, "What good is it?" He thinks the education of black children is unimportant and suggests the congregation be dissolved. From among the Baltimore clergy (even those the sisters believed were on their side) come suggestions that, for black women, being good domestics takes priority over being nuns.

The Sulpician order decides that running the seminary is all it can handle at the moment, leaving no one to spare as chaplain for the Oblates. This means the nuns no longer have Mass in their chapel or an assigned confessor. Adding to the sadness of these days is the death of Sister Mary's close friend, Marie Balas, one of the original Oblates.

To earn rent money and to feed the children at the school, 10 of whom are orphans boarding free, the women take in washing. Sister Mary, along with another nun, accepts employment in the seminary kitchen. In the face of so many difficulties, two other nuns depart the community.

It is at this point that the young Redemptorist, Father Anwander, arrives on the scene and offers to become their chaplain, begging the reluctant Archbishop Eccleston for the privilege. Proving his good intentions, Father Anwander goes from house to house in Baltimore, seeking to enroll more tuition-paying students from the black district as well as asking donations. For the community, which had dwindled to 12 sisters with no postulants or novices in sight and only 20 remaining students, a new period of growth ensues. With Redemptorist support, enrollment increases to 100 day students and 60 boarders, and the number of sisters doubles. Another school is built to accommodate more than 50 boys.

In this pre-Civil War period bitter racial hatred is evidenced in one ugly incident. A national organization called "Know-Nothings" (who are virulently anti-Catholic as well as antiblack) batter down the convent door in a rage, though none of the sisters is injured.

Just about the time the war begins, Father Anwander, after 13 years with them, must leave. Direction of the Oblates is assigned to the Jesuits, who have opened Loyola College near the convent. The new chaplain, Father Miller, sees them through some rough days during the war. When it is over, the nuns again need additional space to take in black children orphaned by the conflict. In 1866 the Jesuits purchase a house for them with the understanding that the sisters, in exchange, will do the college laundry.

Also that year, at the Second Plenary Council of Baltimore, American bishops plead with priests to consecrate themselves to "the service of the colored people."

At various times over the years, Oblates attempt to open schools in other places, including other states, but the traditional problems persist: failure to receive diocesan funding anywhere, black parents too poor to pay tuition and white Catholics unwilling to donate.

When the Jesuit Father Miller suffers deteriorating health, a fourth order, the Josephites, is assigned to direct the nuns. The Josephites are also working in the city's first black parish.

Though it comes a little late, the aging Sister Mary lives long enough to see what the Oblates have dreamed of for years: a public display of support from the hierarchy, Catholics and civic authorities at the order's golden jubilee celebration in 1879.

As a final blessing, Father Anwander—who never lost interest even after he was reassigned—just happens to visit when Sister Mary is on her deathbed. To her joy, he is there to give her the last rites.

AFTERWARD

During Elizabeth Lange's lifetime, the black Oblates were not allowed admission to Catholic colleges. When they needed the special training necessary to teach accredited high school subjects, the women had to rely on clergy and religious from white colleges who were willing to come to the Oblate house and give instruction. The breakthrough came years later, when Villanova, in Pennsylvania, became the first Catholic university to admit them to summer school in 1924. There were by then black Catholic colleges.

Oblates today operate schools in more than a dozen U.S. cities as well as three missions in Costa Rica. (Their mission in Cuba, begun around 1900, was terminated when Fidel Castro came to power.) Their primary concern remains education of the poor, but Oblates are also engaged in day care, campus ministry, pastoral work and adult education.

American nuns of the 19th century preserved the faith of the numerous immigrants who came as political or economic refugees. They did it by imbuing immigrant children with the tenets of Catholicism through the parochial school system pioneered early in the century by Elizabeth Seton.

Anti-Catholic feeling so powerful at the start of that century was considerably mitigated by the equally powerful example of nuns establishing schools which Protestant children might also attend in cities on the frontier and of nuns valiantly nursing victims in epidemics and on Civil War battlefields. In addition, the sisterhood organized and operated a multitude of social services wherever these were lacking.

The strength of the Catholic Church in the United States is due more to nuns than any other single group, athough— witness Elizabeth Lange—recognition has been long in coming.

Jean Donovan

BACKGROUND

In 1908 the Catholic Church in
the United States ceased being classed as mission territory by
the Vatican. In 1911 came the founding of The Catholic
Foreign Mission Society (otherwise known as Maryknoll). A
year later that order opened the first seminary in the country
to train missionaries for work overseas. American sisters,
brothers and priests would now take their turn at serving
mission territories.

Not to be left out, the laity joined in the apostolate at
home, providing social service based on the Gospel through
volunteer lay organizations. Dorothy Day and Peter
Maurin's Catholic Worker Movement and its Hospitality
Houses, and Catherine de Hueck Doherty and Eddie
Doherty's Friendship House in Harlem, for example, were
both conceived in the 1930's. The Legion of Mary, a lay
movement international in scope begun in Dublin in 1921,
found its way to the United States.

Vatican II (1962-1965) set in motion tremendous changes
in the Church. Encompassing both liturgy and a fresh spirit
of openness, it called for looking at what it means to be
Church not only from a Western perspective. One region to
feel the effects most profoundly was Latin America. The real
watershed in the Latin Church came in 1968 when its bishops
met at Medelln, Colombia, and made a commitment to work

for the rights of the poor and to end social injustice, giving impetus to the concept of "liberation theology." (Throughout its history, the Latin Church had traditionally allied itself with the ruling class.)

Maryknoll had been active in the region for some time when, in the mid-1970's, it issued a call for help from the laity in the United States, a need prompted by the sharp drop-off in priestly and religious vocations. The laity responded. Many volunteered for the order's own lay missioner program; in some cases, local churches or dioceses took on projects abroad and availed themselves of Maryknoll's expertise in training missioners for the transcultural experience.

LA LIBERTAD, EL SALVADOR, AUGUST 10, 1979

Arriving in this tropical Pacific Coast town, young Jean Donovan hears the tolling of church bells. She learns that they are being rung in tribute to a local priest who was gunned down at the altar of his church. Parishioners who witnessed the murder say it was committed by three they recognized as policemen.

For Jean, it can hardly be the most promising introduction to her new calling as a lay missioner in Latin America's smallest country. Despite a worsening of violence, the general feeling among North Americans volunteering in El Salvador seems to be that they are relatively safe. The native clergy and native churchworkers involved with the poor are objects of reprisal.

The situation originated a few years previously when priests began identifying with the poor and preaching the need for social justice. In the eyes of the entrenched powers, that was a revolutionary move inevitably leading to class struggle and communism. (In the early 1970's the only communists actually in operation were two small groups of urban guerrillas from middle-class backgrounds.)

Prosperous landowners who, along with the military, controlled the country felt their position threatened. Soon there were death squads aimed at eliminating "communist" priests as well as other "subversives." Those who follow the lead of the Church in the ensuing decade will hold fast to the principle of nonviolent civil disobedience.

Jean has come to this troubled land to join a mission team recruited from her diocese in Cleveland, Ohio. She leaves behind in the States her parents, her brother, close friends (including a special man in her life) and a career job with a prestigious accounting firm.

Both before and after she decides to join the mission team, Jean questions why God has chosen her to make a commitment so far removed from anything she's ever known before. The only answer the 26-year-old woman gets is a deep-down sense that she's made the right choice.

Jean's soul-searching over Christian commitment started in college when she spent her junior year as a foreign-exchange student at the University of Cork in Ireland. There she met a priest, Father Michael Crowley, who had recently returned from missionary work in Peru. He motivated her to volunteer in a Legion of Mary program of visiting the sick and helping the poor in Cork.

Jean returned home, first to graduate, then to earn a master's degree in business. After that she accepted a job with a national firm in Cleveland. Despite the advantages she enjoyed in her rising career, something seemed to be missing. After winning a trip to Europe at an office party, Jean made a return visit to Ireland in January 1977 to talk with her friend, Father Crowley, about the direction of her life. He advised, "You've got everything. You should think about giving a little back to God."

Back in Cleveland, Jean devoted her spare time to work in a diocesan program for inner city youth, an environment considerably removed from her own childhood home in an affluent district of Westport, Connecticut.

In the fall of 1977, in response to Jean's quest for still more to do, a priest mentioned another diocesan project, this one connected with missionary work in El Salvador. The

Cleveland diocese had been providing help to El Salvador since the early 1970's, trying to fill the gap when Salvadoran priests were persecuted and driven out. The diocesan team of volunteers maintained a close working relationship with Maryknoll missionaries in the area.

According to her mother, Jean had talked to a parish priest about her desire to become a missionary after returning from that junior year in Cork. Nevertheless, when Jean's friends and relatives heard what she planned to do, most found the idea of her as a missionary to be at odds with the fun-loving, motorcycle-riding Jean they knew.

To become a lay missioner, Jean was told, one must first be accepted into a four-month training course given by the Maryknolls at their center in Ossining, New York, for these are the professionals in the field. And after that comes three months of intensive Spanish language instruction in Guatemala.

Part of the application process included writing an autobiographical essay. In it, Jean told of the individuals Christ had sent her way to clarify her vocation, and of a serious illness her older brother Michael had which made her realize "how precious life is." Describing two of the most important influences, she wrote: "At times I'm sure my parents both wonder where I got the mission calling. To me it's obvious after having two people such as my parents to grow up with. My father is a gentle man. He has never been afraid to show love. I think I admire this about him best....My mother is a very get-up-and-go person who always seems to have the energy to do something for someone else."

In 1978, along with eight others, Jean was accepted into the course, which extended over the winter and into the spring of 1979. In May she went to Guatemala for Spanish school.

Her first close friend when she joins the team in August will be Ursuline Sister Dorothy Kazel, who has already been in El Salvador for some time. Jean's business background is immediately put to use: She is given charge of the mission accounts. As her first major assignment, she helps in the administration of a food distribution program for a community called Santa Cruz, near the airport. Evenings are given over to coordinating services for the peasants living there—men, women and young children. After laboring from dawn to dusk in the cotton fields of wealthy landowners, they have a supper of beans and tortillas, then go to "church," a wooden shack, where the Bible is read and discussed: the celebration of the Word. Jean experiences unexpected happiness at seeing she can make a difference in the hard lives of the Salvadorans.

In her first months of work, the political situation worsens, violence increases and, with civil war in sight, churchworkers begin making plans for refugee centers.

Spearheading the efforts of the Salvadoran Church is Archbishop Oscar Romero. When appointed to the episcopacy in early 1977 at the age of 59, Romero bore the image of conservative, a choice welcomed by the ruling class. Yet before long his sermons at Sunday morning Mass in San Salvador's cathedral were being applauded in church by the crowds of peasants attending. (The sermons were also broadcast to a larger audience.) When Jean is able to get to the capital, 15 miles from her base, she too applauds Romero's preaching.

Though by nature shy, the archbishop feels called to speak out in defense of the Church and its people, explaining: "There is a terrible situation among the poor—they are crushed in their homes, taken prisoners, made to disappear. They go to jail, are judged falsely and no one pays any attention. I felt I had to be the voice of all those people without a voice."

Leaders of the bloodless military coup in mid-October 1979 promise democratic reforms, but the months that follow prove far from bloodless.

At Christmas Jean's parents, Ray and Pat Donovan, visit, wanting to see things for themselves and to meet their daughter's new friends. Pat remembers their first impression of El Salvador: "The most beautiful place we'd ever seen. Flowers covered the hills." ("Where else would you find roses in December?" Jean had written in her diary.)

The overriding feeling everyone shares is that

missionaries were not at risk, especially not Jean and her coworker Dorothy. Their blond hair and blue eyes identify them as North Americans. They will never be mistaken for Salvadorans as some of the missionaries with darker coloring may be. Any time an errand poses a safety problem, in fact, Jean and Dorothy are sent. No one has yet attacked a foreign woman, and there is no reason to think such an attack is likely.

In retrospect, Pat and her husband realize that Jean took them on the "back route," avoiding worrisome situations. An incident or two will come back to haunt them later, such as the time an armed, drunken soldier pushed his way into their van, demanding a ride somewhere. Jean and Dorothy quietly cautioned the parents: "Don't say a word."

As resistance groups scattered about the countryside prepare to fight against the violence of the National Guard and other government-sponsored forces, the mission team in La Libertad continues ministering to community needs. Determined to preserve an air of normalcy, they teach catechism, give instruction on health matters, dispense food and conduct religious services. Jean takes particular pleasure in organizing a church choir, even though she is teased about her musical abilities.

When her special friend Doug Cable, a doctor she became acquainted with in Cleveland, comes to spend two weeks' vacation in early 1980, she shows him the beaches and other scenic attractions. Only afterward does he realize how, as with her parents' visit, Jean managed to keep him away from the trouble spots.

On March 24 churchworkers are stunned by the news that Archbishop Romero has been shot through the heart while celebrating Mass at the Convent of the Good Shepherd in San Salvador. Bomb blasts and bullets cause still more deaths during the funeral, which Jean attends.

A month later, two Maryknoll nuns, Ita Ford and Carla Piette, arrive to work among the growing number of refugees, for the civil war is intensifying. They set up a refugee center in Chalatenango, a town in the mountainous northeastern province of the country, where guerrilla bands battle with government troops, forcing villagers to flee their homes.

When some of the people from her community of Santa Cruz are found hacked to death, Jean begins to fear for her own safety. The men of the La Libertad mission team add to their work burying the victims of death squads.

On a Sunday evening, July 6, Jean returns from the movies with two friends, young Salvadoran men, one the leader of her church choir. Jean parts company with them to go upstairs to her apartment above the parish school. Just as she reaches it, gunshots ring out. She rushes back down to the street, to the horrifying sight of both friends lying dead.

Though overwhelmed with grief—or because of it—Jean immerses herself in work. Sisters Ita and Carla can use all the help possible at their Maryknoll center in Chalatenango, for the welfare of refugees has become the paramount concern of the Salvadoran archdiocese. Jean and Dorothy start transporting peasants to refugee centers and other safe places as well as taking food and supplies where needed. One night in August, while the two Maryknoll nuns are on an errand of mercy themselves, they meet with an accident. Their jeep is caught up in a flash flood, and though Ita survives, Sister Carla drowns. Maryknoll sends Sister Maura Clarke as her replacement.

At this time, Jean and Dorothy find themselves working more closely than ever with the Chalatenango nuns. Their white Toyota van becomes a familiar sight as it traverses the countryside.

A few weeks after Carla's death, Jean's six-week vacation comes due. First she spends a few days with her parents, then goes on to London to meet Doug, and after that the two go to Ireland for a friend's wedding in Cork. During the days in Cork, Father Crowley as well as Doug try to convince Jean not to return to El Salvador. Others also try to dissuade her when she stops en route back at the Maryknoll Center in Ossining, for all can see that she is a basket case. But Jean keeps telling everyone she has to return, for she has promised the children in El Salvador she will. One priest strongly advises her to think about it for three or four months before making a definite decision.

Jean spends several hours alone in the Maryknoll chapel on her last day there. When she comes out, the nun waiting to drive her to the airport describes her as completely changed from the way she went in, completely at peace with the decision to go back. Jean spends the final days of vacation in Florida with her parents. Jean tells them about the chapel incident: "God straightened the whole thing out for me." She only hopes God will keep her from being tortured. Otherwise, she's willing to die if necessary—then adds quickly that nothing is going to happen. ("She was the old Jeannie—happy," her mother says, remarking that her daughter was always a great one for talking to God like a friend.)

When Jean returns, her coworkers in El Salvador also note a marked change. Peaceful, confident, she is where she belongs.

Most of the last six weeks of her life are spent transporting people and supplies for the Chalatenango center. The churchworkers feel the pressure of surveillance. Threats are made, but still they feel their status as North Americans offers protection to the refugees in their care.

Unaccountably, the week before they die, Jean and Dorothy, who are both animal lovers, give away the dog and cat they have kept at their La Libertad apartment. Other than that, all seems normal.

The last weekend of November, Ita and Maura leave for a four-day conference of Maryknoll Sisters in Nicaragua. Jean and Dorothy attend a reception at which they meet Robert White, the U.S. ambassador, and his wife, and accept an invitation to a dinner party at the San Salvador embassy on December 1. Worried about the women's safety driving after dark, the Whites insist they stay overnight.

On the afternoon of December 2, Jean and Dorothy make the five-mile drive to the airport to pick up two of the nuns returning from the conference in Nicaragua. They return to meet an early evening flight carrying Ita Ford and Maura Clarke. It is dark when the four leave the airport. They will never be seen alive again.

The following day Jean's parents receive notification that she is missing. On December 4 their worst fears are confirmed: Jean's body and those of her three coworkers are discovered in a ditch in a secluded spot. They have been sexually assaulted, then shot.

AFTERWARD

Two weeks before the killings, Ronald Reagan, president-elect at the time, sent emissaries to the Salvadoran government. They promised that, once Reagan became president, human rights violations would no longer be a factor in determining aid. The government would receive all the guns and other help it needed.

Despite protests from Ambassador White (who was soon the ex-ambassador), a cover-up persisted in shielding Salvadoran officials responsible for ordering the killings. Finally, in 1984, five National Guard soldiers were found guilty of the actual shooting.

Father Crowley of Cork was in the habit of telling his Legion of Mary group: "It's better to *do* something than to give up something." He would later say that Jean was the first to take him up on this. As her destiny would have it, however, in doing something, Jean gave up something, too: the ultimate, her life.

Into the 21st Century

Looking Ahead

This story of women in the Church has taken us across the map from Christianity's origins in the Near East to Europe to the Western Hemisphere. Now we approach the Southern Hemisphere where, by the 21st century, a predicted two-thirds of Christendom will be represented by people of the Third World.

The martyrdom of Jean Donovan and the other three churchwomen calls our attention to the Church in the Third World, reminiscent in its vitality of the early Church and its evangelizers and martyrs. In the basic ecclesial communities of Latin America and elsewhere, we see a repeat of history: full participation in ministry by laypersons—much as in apostolic times.

In the universal Church, not just in the Third World, we see the laity sharing increasingly in ministry. This participation is, in fact, the most visible sign today in our faith. In word and in deed, laity as well as religious proclaim the Good News. Laity means men *and* women. Together. And that is the Best News.